BARBRA STREISAND

BARBRA STREISAND

David Bret

First published in the USA by Unanimous Ltd
254–258 Goswell Road, London EC1V 7RL

Series Editor: Martin Aston
Text Editor: Ian Fitzgerald
Project Editor: Nicola Birtwisle

ISBN: 1-56649-171-1

Distributed by Welcome Rain Distribution LLC

Printed in Italy

1 2 3 4 5 6 7 8 9

CONTENTS

INTRODUCTION

When asked by a reporter if she could explain *why* she had become so successful, Barbra Streisand once replied, neither tongue-in-cheek nor boastful: 'The only way I can account for it is that whatever ability other performers have, I must have it plus. On stage I'm a cross between a washerwoman and a princess. I'm a bit coarse, a bit low, a bit vulgar and a bit ignorant. But I'm also part princess – sophisticated, elegant and controlled. I can appeal to everybody, I guess.'

In common with most of her female counterparts, Streisand is renowned for being fearsome and fearless – no wonder, she has been more or less compelled to make it to the top alone. And, of course, success of her magnitude all too often breeds contempt. Many of her co-stars and directors profess to disliking her, largely on account of her niggling insistence upon getting everything absolutely right. She is known to have argued persistently over a certain camera angle or arc-light which she said highlighted her bad side (her right profile), and for often threatening to walk out of a production. She would change lines, sometimes an entire scene, if it did not 'feel' right – even scenes she herself was not appearing in.

Though by no means as ferocious as a Davis or a Crawford, while shooting *Funny Girl* Streisand is said to have put William Wyler, one of Hollywood's greatest directors, through his paces by challenging his every instruction so that when the production wound up he handed her his famous megaphone and suggested that she might be better directing a film herself. Fifteen years later, she did.

As a superbly gifted *chanteuse*, Streisand has few equals – none living – and can sing just about anything. According to Marlene Dietrich, Streisand could convincingly sing 'The contents of the telephone directory, if someone asked her to.' And the older she gets, the better the voice becomes. As an ambassadress and tireless campaigner for political and social issues, notably the fight against AIDS, she reigns supreme. This is her story.

Acknowledgements
Writing this book would not have been possible had it not been for the inspiration, criticisms and love of that select group of individuals, my true family and *autre coeur*: Barbara, Irene Bevan, Marlene Dietrich, Dorothy Squires, Roger Normand *que vous dormez en paix*; René and Lucette Chevalier, Jacqueline Danno, Hélène Delavault, Tony Griffin, Betty Paillard, Annick Roux, Terry Sanderson, John and Anne Taylor, François and Madeleine Vals, Caroline Clerc, Charley Marouani. Especial thanks to my agent, David Bolt...and to my wife Jeanne, still the keeper of my soul. Books about Streisand are legion, some good, some bad. Accuracy comes with James Spada's *Streisand, The Intimate Biography* (1995, Crown Publishers Inc.), and Anne Edwards' excellent *Streisand* (1996, Weidenfeld and Nicholson), whereas gossips and drama queens will love Ernest W. Cunningham's *The Ultimate Barbra* (1998, Renaissance Books). I humbly thank my editor, Martin Aston, for his time and patience.

'La vie sans amis est comme un jardin sans fleurs.'

ONE

THE STORY

Hers was not a privileged childhood. Neither was it a happy one. She was born Barbara Joan Streisand in the East Flatbush section of Brooklyn, New York, on 24 April 1942. Always an ungainly child (she never knew her father, Emmanuel, who died aged just thirty-five from respiratory failure when she was sixteen months old), she was constantly reminded of her unattractiveness, notably her wide, melon-shaped mouth and large, misshapen nose, by her stepfather who most inappropriately went by the name of Louis Kind. He only married her mother, Diana, when compelled to do so by Diana's pregnancy. Streisand's sister, Rosalind, was born in January 1950, two weeks after the wedding, increasing the brood to three – Barbara's older brother, Sheldon Jay, had been born in 1935. Many years later, promoting one of her films in London, Streisand would say of her obnoxious parent, 'He did not physically abuse me, as in the film *Nuts*, but mentally he did and my mother allowed it to happen.'

Barbara was seven when her mother remarried, and in photographs taken at the time surprisingly resembles her soon to be alter-ego, Fanny Brice – as if destiny has already decided that they would one day be conjoined. And like many desperately miserable youngsters, she soon began searching for an escape from the drudgery of her home life, where one of her few pleasures was the 'new-fangled' television she was occasionally allowed to watch and enthuse over the high-rating variety shows presented by the likes of Ed Sullivan, Steve Allen and Milton Berle. School was no less of an ordeal, even for a girl with an IQ of 124. She attended Brooklyn's Erasmus High, a somewhat privileged but snooty establishment, where the taunts from some of the other pupils were infinitely worse than the ones she suffered at home – particularly after they learned that Louis Kind's favourite appellation for his daughters was 'Beauty and the Beast'. Barbara was, of course, the latter.

Barbara's first real treading of the boards, as opposed to the usual end of term concerts and plays, occurred in June 1957, one month after her mother had been granted a legal separation from Kind on grounds of cruelty. John Hale, the artistic director of New York's Malden Bridge Playhouse, was recruiting apprentices of seventeen years and above for summer stock, to be employed in all aspects of theatrical work. Barbara added two years to her age, talked her mother into paying the $300 fee, and embarked on what were arguably the happiest three months of her life so far. She was initially put to work behind the scenes – scrubbing floors, running errands, making the tea – though when she did get round to actual acting, she made a point of making sure she was noticed. One local newspaper observed of her only speaking part, in an obscure piece entitled *The Desk Set*, 'Barbara Streisand turns in a fine performance as the office vamp. *Down*, boys!'

A few weeks after her term at Malden Bridge, Barbara successfully applied for a one-year apprenticeship at the Cherry Lane Theatre, in Manhattan's Greenwich Village, working several evenings a week and at weekends. The bohemian way of life here, akin to the earlier Existentialists of Paris' Left Bank, suited her well and also brought out her zaniness. Tired of being labelled ugly – which truthfully she was not – Barbara opted to draw even more attention to herself by wearing garish make-up and black clothes. She became friendly with Alan Miller, the outfit's drama coach, who accepted her into his Method-inspired workshop, and here she fell in love for the first time with a twenty-three-year-old actor named Roy Scott, a relationship that was soon scuppered by Mrs Streisand. Her daughter was, after all, still under age.

Barbara stayed on with the Cherry Tree after graduating from Erasmus High in January 1959, and celebrated her new-found freedom by moving to Manhattan, sharing a tiny apartment with a friend. To make ends meet, she took on any number of ad-hoc jobs to support herself and pay for acting lessons – cleaning, babysitting, and, for nine months, full-time employment as a printing company clerk. The seed for the mighty singing career was sown inadvertently early in 1960 whilst Barbara was working part-time as an usher at New York's Lunt-Fontaine Theatre. The show was *The Sound Of Music* with Mary Martin. Within days she had memorised all the musical numbers, and when a room-mate overheard her singing one of these, Barbara was persuaded to audition for a part in the show's chorus for when it went on the road. She did not get the part, but she followed the producer's advice and began looking for work in nightclubs in and around Greenwich Village.

Exactly why Barbara stuck with Greenwich Village instead of travelling further afield is not known, though it certainly began her life-long affinity with the gay community which thrives to this day. Urged by another friend – Barry Denne, who briefly became her lover – she entered a talent contest at the Lion, a seedy gay club at 62 West 9th Street, and with a scorching performance of Harold Arlen's 'A Sleepin' Bee' brought the house down and walked off with the $50 prize. What she did not know was that the audiences were notorious for sending up those brave enough to take the stage – particularly a gawky-looking young woman bedecked in purple ostrich plumes and wearing a shoe in her hair because she had been unable to remove the fake jewel from its heel and strap. No one laughed, however, and she was invited to return the next week to 'defend' her title – something she did several times until the manager asked her to step down and give someone else a chance.

For a while, Barbara stayed on at the Lion – as cloakroom attendant – before auditioning for a short season at the slightly more upmarket Bon Soir Club, on 8th Street. She was so nervous that she forgot to remove the chewing gum from her mouth – no problem, for she spat it out and stuck it to the microphone, which of course brought mingled hoots of laughter and derision. Then, after holding the clientele spellbound with 'A Sleepin' Bee', she pulled a hideous face and ripped straight into a two-octave rendition of 'Who's Afraid Of The Big Bad Wolf?' which had everyone genuinely splitting their sides. The establishment took her on at $125 a week, told her to keep up the chewing gum routine and throw in a few Yiddish jokes, and she opened on 9 September 1960 supporting wacky comedienne Phyllis Diller. The visiting press virtually ignored the star of the show. The *New York Sun* called Barbara 'the find of the year', while one of the city's most acerbic critics, Dorothy Kilgallen, enthused, 'She's never had a singing lesson in her life, doesn't know how to walk, dress or take a bow, but she *projects* well enough to bring the house down.'

Within weeks, Barbara had engaged her first manager, Ted Rozar – though he would soon be replaced by her Svengali, Marty Erlichman, who is with her to this day. She also slightly amended her first name – from now on she would only ever be known as *Barbra*. In February 1961 she made her radio debut in Detroit and that April, shortly before her nineteenth birthday, came her first television appearance, alongside Phyllis Diller on the *Jack Parr Show*. After this she returned to the Bon Soir, took two weeks off to appear at a Jewish nightclub in Ottawa, and appeared on *P.M. East*, the television chat show hosted by national favourite Mike Wallace – earning such rave reviews, particularly after duetting 'I Wish I Were In Love Again' with Mickey Rooney, that she would be invited back twelve times over the next year. Inevitably, this mass exposure led to her first true theatrical audition, for a part in an off-Broadway oddity entitled *Harry Stoones*. She got the part.

The curtain went up on 21 October 1961, but in a city where adverse criticism can close even a good play on its opening night – which is exactly what happened in this instance – Barbra's excitement soon turned to despondency, and for several weeks she returned to the gay clubs of Greenwich Village. Then, in a wholly unprecedented reversal of fortune she attracted huge critical acclaim – and the New York Critics' Award – for her portrayal of Yetta Tessye Marmelstein, the kooky spinster in David Merrick's production of Harold Rome and Arthur Laurents' *I Can Get It For You Wholesale*, which opened on Broadway on 22 March 1962. She made the most spectacular entrance – shooting onto the stage in a swivel chair, eyes crossed and arms and legs akimbo, a pencil sticking out of her beehive hairdo – and had the audience in stitches before uttering a word. Later, her big production number, 'Miss Marmelstein', received a three-minute ovation. One notice, penned by *Theatre Arts'* John Simon, assured her that this would not be her last. 'Gifted with a face that shuttles between those of a tremulous young Borzoi and a fatigued Talmudic scholar,' Simon observed, 'this girl can also sing the lament of the unreconstructed drudge with the clarion peal of an *Un*-Liberty Bell!'

Similarly applauded by Simon's colleagues, inside twenty-four hours Barbra Streisand had become the toast of Broadway and would henceforth mostly play Jewish characters who were like herself: witty, difficult, strong-willed by the way of adversity, hard-edged, utterly unpredictable, and, more frequently than not, hilariously madcap. And with success there came personal joy. The hero of the piece, set in the late 1930s, is garment industry entrepreneur Harry Bogen, whose ruthless quest for power alienates him with everyone he holds dear. Playing Bogen was twenty-three-year-old Elliott Gould, unknown at the time. Good-looking in a mournful sort of way, Gould and Barbra hit it off at once, and he moved into her tiny one-room apartment.

The success of *Wholesale* pushed Barbra's manager into trying to secure her a recording contract – an invidious quest, apparently, because the major companies initially dismissed her singing style as 'too specialised'. She did appear on the *Wholesale* cast album, cut one week after the premiere, and also on the 25th anniversary edition album of Rome's first Broadway hit, *Pins and Needles*, but it was her increasing television guest slots on *P.M. East* which resulted in her being eventually approached by Columbia.

Barbra's initial contract with Columbia – a one-year, two-album deal which she signed on 1 October 1962, afforded her complete control over her material, arrangements, musicians and even studio personnel – unusual in those days. Though with just $20,000 advance royalties for each album until she had proved her worth, Barbra's remuneration was considerably lower than it might have been elsewhere. Before the albums, however, she was asked to cut a single. Her soon-to-be signature tune, 'Happy Days Are Here Again' was for some reason distributed only in New York, but caused such a fuss that its successor, 'My Colouring Book' – a hit in Europe for Greek star Nana Mouskouri – sold a more than modest 65,000 copies and earned her a guest spot on Ed Sullivan's huge-rating *Tonight* show. From now on, she would not look back.

Barbra's intention was that her debut album should comprise a recital at her favourite club, the Bon Soir, but the poor acoustics and rowdy audience participation put paid to this and she entered Columbia's Studio A on 23 January 1963. *The Barbra Streisand Album* hit the stores one month later, and by April would peak at Number 8 on the *Billboard* chart. Meanwhile, following the closure of *Wholesale* the previous

December, and despite some serious competition from – amongst others – Juliet Prowse and Shirley Maclaine, Barbra had been chosen to play Fanny Brice in Jules Styne and Bob Merrill's new musical, *Funny Girl*. Although Anne Bancroft had been originally due to take the role, and had dropped out, Barbra seemed the ideal choice to portray the performer to whom she had often been compared. The only catch was that her television commitments and album promotion meant that she would not be able to open for another year.

In May, Barbra appeared on Dinah Shore's television show, and after her most prestigious season guest slot so far, supporting Benny Goodman at the Basin Street East, she sang for President Kennedy at the Press Correspondents' Dinner – almost an equivalent of the British Royal Variety Show. In the June she recorded the eleven songs for *The Second Barbra Streisand Album* – released at the end of August. This would prove even more successful than the first, reaching Number 2 on the *Billboard* chart, and contained what must surely be *the* definitive rendition of 'I Stayed Too Long At The Fair'. Then she played sell-out seasons in Chicago, Las Vegas and Los Angeles' fabled Cocoanut Grove, at the latter breaking the box office record set by Judy Garland in 1958. Each evening she received a standing ovation, but never returned to the stage for an encore – something which saw her criticised somewhat by the largely celebrity audience.

At around this time, Barbra gave up her tiny flat and moved to her new home – a sumptuous duplex near New York's Central Park which had formerly belonged to composer Lorenz Hart. On 13 September 1963 – an 'unlucky' Friday – she married Elliott Gould in a spur-of-the-moment ceremony in mid-tour Carson City, Nevada, and even here she could not resist clowning around – or was she being serious as some said? – by changing one of her marriage vows to 'Love, honour and feed'. Such a vow, in retrospect, was not far off the mark, for the union would be doomed almost from the start. Gould, constantly referred to in show business circles as 'Mr Streisand', would enjoy a moderately successful stage and film career, but not without always finding himself walking in the shadow of his wife's sun and, it is alleged, frequently reminded of the fact.

On 26 March 1964, following tryouts in Boston and Philadelphia, *Funny Girl* opened at New York's Winter Garden Theater, the scene of so many of Fanny Brice's own triumphs. Brice (1891–1951) had been a brash, larger-than-life character. The Ziegfeld Follies' biggest star between 1910 and 1925, though far from attractive and possessed of a poor but plaintive singing voice, her tremendous personality had endeared her to millions. In 1912 she had met and fallen in love with Nick Arnstein, a handsome, sophisticated con man with whom she had lived openly until their marriage in 1918. Throughout the nine years of this extremely volatile union, apart from the two spells he had spent in prison for embezzlement, Arnstein had tricked Brice out of almost every dollar she had earned. Shortly before her death, Brice had dictated her memoirs into a tape recorder, but her family had considered these too racy for publication. They had eventually been destroyed by her son-in-law, film producer Ray Stark, and *Funny Girl* was to be his 'cleaned up' – if not inaccurate – tribute to this talented, very unusual woman. Barbra was ably supported by Jean Stapleton and Kay Medford, and Sydney Chaplin (Charlie's son) played Nick Arnstein. The score contained songs which had been launched by Brice – 'I'd Rather Be Blue Over You', 'Second Hand Rose' – and others which Barbra would make her own: 'People', 'Don't Rain On My Parade'. Brice's signature tune, 'My Man', had been introduced to American audiences as 'Mon Homme' in 1923 by French singer Mistinguett. However, she had not liked it much and sold the rights for a paltry $100. Her version of the number has subsequently sold a million copies and remains the best, despite Streisand's powerhouse performance.

The rehearsals for *Funny Girl* had apparently been as fraught as any episode in Brice's own life. When signed for the show,

Barbra's salary had been set at $1,500 a week, not bad for a comparative novice, but her rapidly escalating success in the year which had elapsed between then and the tryouts now brought about a demand for $7,500 a week, a chauffeured limousine, personal assistant and hairdresser – and as much food as she and Elliott Gould could eat. An uneasy compromise was reached wherein she would be paid $5,000, without the trappings. On top of this there had been innumerable script changes, temper tantrums and threatened sackings and walkouts. By all accounts, in common with Brice, Streisand also had an affinity for out-cursing even the best of them. The press also reported that Streisand and thirty-eight-year-old Sydney Chaplin were having an affair.

It was all worth it, of course. The show was in two halves: Fanny the teenage hopeful, then as the institution she became – minus the alcoholic, hedonistic decline, but with one major difference. Her 'impersonator' had readily asserted, long before heralding the intermission with 'Don't Rain On My Parade', that she was *already* a far greater superstar than Brice had ever been. As was later pointed out by her biographer, James Spada, 'It was the start of the Streisand cult'.

The reviews for the show were superlative, though of course there had to be a handful of detractors forever ranting over Barbra's 'striking resemblance' to Fanny Brice, something she might have had during her youth, though certainly not now. She was vigorously defended against these by the *New York Morning Telegraph*'s Whitney Bolton: 'when she is a clown, she is an all-out clown…confronted by a romance that could lead to more intimate association, she managed first to josh the whole idea, then to hurl herself at their relationship and take it whole to her heart. Miss Streisand, also like Fanny, is no pretty girl. She does not need to be and never will. That talent will flame for a long time. *Much* longer than the vapid accident of beauty.'

The affair with Sydney Chaplin proved short-lived, and

though he and Barbra ended up loathing each other, he perse-
vered with the show until the summer of 1965, when he was
replaced by Johnny Desmond. In the meantime, what looked
like being a very long Broadway run did not deter Barbra from
her other projects. In September 1964 her fourth studio album,
People, topped the *Billboard* chart – a sizeable feather in her
cap, for it knocked the Beatles' *A Hard Day's Night* off the top
spot. A few months later she signed a contract with CBS for a
staggering $5 million to make five 60-minute television spe-
cials. There were also those occasions when the curtain stayed
down on *Funny Girl* so that Barbra could participate in star-
studded galas such as President Johnson's inaugural command
performance on 18 January 1965, and a benefits concert on
4 April, attended by Martin Luther King, which raised
$150,000 for civil rights groups.

The one-woman television special, *My Name Is Barbra*,
filmed in monochrome and televised in March, attracted 40 per
cent of the nation's viewers, making Barbra a household name
for those who did not know her already. 'She is so great, it is
shocking,' enthused the usually reserved *United Press
International*. The song-and-dance numbers were staged and
choreographed by Joe Layton, who had recently won a Tony
award for his work on Richard Rodgers' *No Strings*. In the
first, Barbra was seen dressed as a child amongst huge props
and looked about seven. She spoke dryly of how everyone
poked fun at her by calling her 'Big Beak', then escorted the
audience through a tour of the Bergdorf Goodman department
store where, while trying on a weird assortment of clothes, she
sang songs associated with Fanny Brice and her contempo-
raries. This first show closed in spectacular fashion – a single
spotlight which picked her out, Piaf-like, against a black back-
drop, whilst she sang standards such as 'Why Did I Choose
You?'

My Name Is Barbra was awarded six Emmy nominations and
won five of these, including the much-coveted Outstanding

Individual Achievement By An Actor Or Performer. Barbra's continuing success, however, had begun placing a strain on her already shaky marriage – as she went from strength to strength, Elliott Gould hardly worked at all that past year. Indeed, when he eventually landed a part in the Broadway musical *Drat! The Cat!* in October, Barbra was reputed to have invested $100,000 of her own money to keep the production afloat – if so, it was a wasted effort, for the show survived less than a week. On the positive side, however, it gave her one of her best songs – 'He Touched Me' was included on the second of the two albums released to tie in with the television special, and, perhaps solely because of Barbra, was not assigned to oblivion along with other material for the Gould revue.

Barbra was nominated for a Tony for *Funny Girl*, but this award went to Carol Channing for *Hello Dolly!* She continued with the show, frequently declaring that she was tired with the monotony of doing the same thing every evening, until 26 December, when she stepped down to prepare for the three months' London run with Michael Craig. (The New York production would continue, playing to less packed, less enthusiastic audiences with Mimi Hines in the title role until the middle of 1967.) It was during this final performance that Barbra sang 'My Man' for the first time, reducing both the audience and herself to tears when they showed their appreciation by standing to link arms and sing 'Auld Lang Syne'.

Before travelling to London, Barbra taped her second television special, *Colour Me Barbra*, for CBS. Because it was shot in colour, in 1966 still innovative, there were technical hitches besides the usual temperamental explosions which were by now part of the Streisand package. One of the programme's scenes featured several animals (including an anteater!), some of which went out of control under the scorching arc-lights. Barbra was especially distressed when a baby penguin she had taken to died. Determined to get as much of the tiresome filming out of the way, she was reported at one stage to have kept everyone working for thirty-two hours without sleep – if the star could do it, then so could they! Perhaps the most exquisite, lasting image from the production occurred when Barbra put her so-called Egyptian profile to good use by appearing as an exact replica of Queen Nefertiti, posing next to her famous bust in the Philadelphia Museum. And *Colour Me Barbra* was a brilliant piece of show business history, despite the misgivings expressed by some of the critics. Fortunately, perhaps, she would not be around to read some of the reviews after the show was aired at the end of March 1966, especially the one in *Time* magazine which pontificated: 'The show proved that one full hour of Streisand's particularly nasal voice is about forty-five minutes too much.'

Barbra arrived in London on 20 March, one week after her husband, who had travelled ahead of her to find them somewhere to live – after a few days at the Savoy, they moved to a £1,000 a week flat in Ennismore Gardens. Gould had been offered the part of Nick Arnstein, only to have turned it down, it is said, for fear of being accused of nepotism. The press, who knew very little about him, dubbed him 'Mr Streisand' the same as everyone else and in any case were only interested in his famous spouse. 'Rarely in the whole bedazzled history of live and lusty entertainment has one box of assorted vocal chords been awaited with such pent-up, electrifying excitement,' declared the *Daily Mirror*.

This particular box of vocal chords saw red, however, the instant she entered the Prince of Wales Theatre. Declaring the star dressing room unfit for an artiste who had been setting Broadway alight for the past nineteen months, Barbra refused to set foot in the place again until it had been completely refurbished. The management complied, knocking two rooms into one and even filling it with antique furniture.

The London premiere of *Funny Girl* took place on 13 April, and Barbra lived up to everyone's expectations. *The Times* called her 'a redeeming presence', the *Daily Sketch* 'the most phenomenal creature of strange chemistry ever to set foot on a stage', the *Daily Mail* 'the heart, the sound *and* the music' of *Funny Girl*. Over the course of the next fourteen weeks anyone who was anyone simply had to felicitate this 'new' singing sensation after the show. Some visitors to the dressing room were made welcome, others not. At times La Streisand could be insufferably tetchy and, to those she found boring, downright rude. Her alleged comments to British star Tommy Steele and Princess Margaret remain unprintable, whereas her meeting with Sophia Loren brought out a classic one-liner. When the Italian actress commented how *she* would give anything to have such a remarkable voice, Barbra glanced at the voluptuous figure and features straight out of a Botticelli painting and cracked in her best Brooklyn, 'If I could look like you, I wouldn't even wanna *talk!*'

Despite her staggering success with the role, however, Barbra decided that two years of Fanny Brice was more than enough, and in London on 16 July – her 900th performance of *Funny Girl* – she announced that she was calling it a day. She told the press before leaving England two days later that she would be back with another show – what they, her legion of fans and she herself did not know was that she would never set foot on the legitimate stage again. She was also pregnant: on 29 December 1966 her son Jason Emmanuel was born at New York's Mount Sinai Hospital.

In 1965, Barbra signed a $250,000 contract with producer Ray Stark for the film version of *Funny Girl*, since which time he had been trying to sell the project to one of the major Hollywood studios. Several had been willing to buy – though not with Streisand in the title role. Applying the still widely practised adage that stage stars rarely transferred well to the big screen (which was why Audrey Hepburn had been cast in *My Fair Lady*, and not Julie Andrews, who had created the role), two of the main contenders had been, as with the New York show, Shirley Maclaine and Juliet Prowse, the former because she was possessed of 'the Brice mug', hardly a compliment! A third proposition had been Mary Martin, who had subsequently been discounted for not being Jewish. Stark, however, had proved persuasive and Barbra subsequently hit the jackpot – a three-picture deal with Columbia for *Funny Girl, Hello Dolly!* and *On A Clear Day You Can See Forever,* with a combined budget of $35 million – effectively making her the only performer in Hollywood aside from Elvis Presley to have signed such a deal *before* facing a camera.

Barbra swept into Hollywood to face her movie peers at a $1 million reception organised by Ray Stark on 14 May 1967. Virtually every major star in town at the time was invited along, with dozens of important studio executives and personnel, press photographers, ace reporters and gossip columnists – and she kept them waiting for over two hours. She further upset many of these luminaries with her subsequent off-the-cuff comments. She declared that she was renting Greta Garbo's former home because it and its occupant had had a class so lacking in the film capital, whereas most of the people she had met here so far were little more than images and commodities – all perfectly true, of course. Then, when asked if she was thinking of settling down in Hollywood now that she had been offered an extremely lucrative deal, Barbra snarled that she definitely did *not* wish to raise her son in a town where a person was judged by the size of their swimming pool. Coming from a woman renowned for fearlessly expressing her opinions, this was too much, particularly when it emerged that she had recently netted an alleged $100,000 for a single concert in Newport, Rhode Island.

The original director of *Funny Girl* had been Sidney Lumet, of *Twelve Angry Men* fame, but after only a few months of pre-production he was replaced by William Wyler, a feisty, picky man nicknamed 'Once-More Wyler' on account of the inordinate number of takes he would order before being satisfied with a particular scene. Wyler was thought of as a good choice for

Barbra because in a lengthy career he had handled some of Hollywood's most trying stars, notably Bette Davis, with whom he had made *Jezebel, The Little Foxes* and *The Letter*. Equally famously, he had directed *Ben Hur*. Herbert Ross, who besides working on *I Can Get It For You Wholesale* had choreographed *Carmen Jones* and Cliff Richard's *The Young Ones* and *Summer Holiday*, was brought in to direct the film's sixteen musical tableaux. The director of photography was Harry Stradling, the British cinematographer whose many credits included *The Pirate, Easter Parade* and *Guys And Dolls*.

As with virtually every Streisand project by now, production problems were legion, though not always her fault. Barbra, just about the only star *not* to have been exasperated by Wyler's multitude of takes, had refused to submit to the obligatory screen test, so Harry Stradling entered the scenario with little idea of how he would light her, given the fact that she had declared certain facial angles taboo. The biggest dilemma centred around Sidney Lumet's choice for Nick Arnstein, Omar Sharif, again through no fault of the actor. Sharif, the star of *Doctor Zhivago* who would be playing a Jew in the film, was Egyptian by birth and Lebanese by descent. Barbra was Jewish – as was almost everyone else involved in the movie – and the Middle East was about to enter the six-day Arab-Israeli War. William Wyler, also Jewish, was urged to fire Sharif, or risk an international incident, but stunned everyone by refusing to do so, declaring that America was supposed to be an unprejudiced society. Barbra defended Wyler's decision by telling a press conference that theatrical folk did not judge each other by way of creed, but by their talent. The comment, augmented by the rumours that she and Sharif were lovers already, resulted in every one of her films being banned in the Arab world, an embargo which holds to this day.

On 17 June, smack in the middle of this political furore, Barbra gave a free concert in New York's Central Park which was filmed and recorded for future release. A crowd of 50,000 was anticipated, but 135,000 turned up, presenting a nightmare – only hours before she was due to go on stage, Barbra's security had received a death threat from the Palestine Liberation Organisation on account of her support for Israel during the Middle East conflict. The concert, fortunately, went without a hitch. Many of the Streisand classics were there, and the crowd were encouraged to sing along with 'Second Hand Rose'. In some songs, not unexpectedly, she sounded tremulous, forgetting the words to two of them on account of her nerves. Indeed, the fear she experienced throughout the evening is said to have stayed with her for another twenty years, which was how long it took her to get around to performing live again in New York.

At a time when pop culture was at its peak and many thought the age of the 'good old-fashioned musical' dead and gone, *Funny Girl* proved one of the most successful films of the 1960s, grossing over $25 million at the US box office alone and enabling Barbra to scoop her first Oscar as Best Actress (an award she shared with Katharine Hepburn for *The Lion In Winter*). As Fanny Brice she really does pull out all the stops, in spite of her apprehension over her right-side profile, looking far more glamorous than anyone had ever given her credit for. 'Let's dispose at once of the ugly duckling myth,' Pauline Kael wrote in her *New Yorker* column in response to colleagues who had suggested that the film served as a prime example that one did not have to be attractive to get on in the world, 'The message of Barbra Streisand in *Funny Girl* is that *talent* is beauty.'

She also sounded better than Brice ever did, from the first 'Hello, gorgeous!' through to the 'My Man' finale, though the way she attacked this was regarded by some vaudeville enthusiasts (including Jule Styne, who had known Brice and thought such a song made her appear erroneously self-pitying) as way too raucous and over the top. Both Brice and Mistinguett had recited it simply, in the lower register, but again, technically, neither had been legitimate singers, but rather *interprètes*. She was also a good deal funnier and almost tearfully wistful when portraying those more turbulent moments which in real life had frequently seen Brice on the brink of suicide. Even the usually hypercritical *Newsweek* could only wildly enthuse, 'Miss Streisand has matured into a complete performer and delivered the most accomplished, original and enjoyable musical-comedy performance that has ever been captured on film.'

There were no doubts as to who would be taking the lead in Jerry Herman's *Hello, Dolly!*, even though Twentieth Century-Fox was inundated with complaints from angry Carol Channing fans who thought she should have been given the part. There was a point during the shooting of *Funny Girl* where, though Barbra had been contracted to play wealthy widow Dolly Levi, she could have been replaced by the older actress, but now neither Channing nor her Broadway successors (including stalwarts Betty Grable and Ginger Rogers) were given a look-in, despite the fact that these were of an age more suited to the ubiquitous meddling matron, the mainstay of Thornton Wilder's stageplay, *The Matchmaker* – portrayed in the 1958 film by Shirley Booth. At twenty-six, Barbra certainly was far too young for the role, but with its fondness for rewriting history, Hollywood was prepared to overlook such a 'minor' detail in exchange for the now monetarily proven Streisand wit, voice and charisma – characteristics none of her older rivals possessed with such innate abundance. Barbra was loaned out to the studio for the $24 million production, and when she cracked that she wanted one of her favourite stars, Gene Kelly, to direct, no one objected, though within a very short time the pair would be expressing their loathing of each other. Neither did the studio baulk at Barbra's inordinate salary demands – $750,000 plus a share of the profits.

Hello, Dolly! was given a sterling support cast, with top honours going to screen-heavy-turned-comedian Walter Matthau for his portrayal of surly, tight-fisted love interest Horace Vandergelder, a role which could not have been better cast.

Other parts went to Tommy Tune, British actor Michael Crawford – a relative newcomer to musicals in those days – and Marianne McAndrew. There was also a delightful cameo from Louis Armstrong, whose version of the title track earned him a world-wide hit. Satchmo duets with Barbra during a café sequence.

From the word go, Barbra experienced immense personal problems with Walter Matthau, an experienced actor who seems to have been unable to relate to the fact that artistically, he was now considered the subordinate of a film novice (*Funny Girl* had not yet been released) only half his age (newspapers across the United States reported Matthau's first confrontation with Streisand wherein he had yelled at her, 'You might be the singer in this picture, but *I'm* the actor. You haven't got the talent of a butterfly's fart!'). Also widely publicised was Matthau's put-down by studio head Richard Zanuck. When Matthau complained that Barbra's opinionating was putting his health at risk, Zanuck sarcastically responded, 'I'd like to help you, but the film isn't called *Hello, Walter!*'

Shooting of *Hello, Dolly!* had taken just thirteen weeks, and though it required the minimum of editing, its release had to be delayed until December 1969: a term of the screen rights contract dictated that the film would have to stay on the shelf until the closure of the Broadway show. It was well worth the wait, for it won three Oscars (Score Adaptation, Art Direction, Sound). In spite of this and the superlative reviews – the *New York Times* called Barbra 'a national treasure' – Twentieth Century Fox deemed it a semi-failure because it only recovered $15 million of its huge budget from its first box office season.

In February 1969, the press announced that Barbra and Elliott Gould had entered into a trial separation, news that the show business fraternity had been expecting for some time – though she declared that they were still and always would remain friends. They certainly gave the impression of the proverbially happily married couple two months later at the

Oscars ceremony. It would take them another two years to file for divorce when, to expedite matters, the papers were filed in the Dominican Republic. Soon afterwards Gould would marry Jenny Bogart (daughter of director Paul), his girlfriend who had announced her pregnancy in the midst of the Goulds' marital strife.

Barbra's third film in her initial Hollywood contract was yet another Broadway show – Alan Jay Lerner and Burton Lane's *On A Clear Day You Can See Forever*, which saw her in a semi-comic vein working with her classiest co-star of all, Franco-Italian heart-throb Yves Montand – who, it must be said, carried the vehicle from start to finish. Montand plays the psychiatrist who puts the Streisand character, Daisy Gamble, into a hypnotic trance to cure her smoking addiction. During this she is transported back to Regency England, becoming Lady Melinda Tentrees, who seduces a young lord (John Richardson). There are complications, however, when the psychiatrist also falls in love with her – not in her present life but while she is Melinda. The Regency scenes were shot in England at the Brighton Pavilion, the stunning period costumes were designed by Cecil Beaton, and this time there were no personality clashes. Barbra and Montand, the most genial of actors, got along extremely well and she adored director Vincente Minnelli, formerly married to her idol, Judy Garland. In Barbra's eyes, anyone who had loved Garland simply had to be exemplary and she was distressed when the great star died towards the end of shooting.

The presence of the legendary Minnelli, however, did little to prevent the film being savaged by the critics. Offering its usual Streisand put-down, *Time* declared that in one scene she looked 'like Jerry Lewis in drag'. Though it showed a healthy profit, the film would prove nowhere near as successful at the box office as its predecessors.

Fortunately Barbra's albums, released at alarmingly regular intervals, were selling like hot cakes. *Simply Streisand* and

A Christmas Album had come out at the end of 1967. The former, a collection of straight-sung ballads, contained 'Stout-Hearted Men', from Sigmund Romberg's *The New Moon*, though Barbra's interpretation leaned more heavily on her Mae West imitation than the MacDonald and Eddy original, and soon became that season's gay anthem in clubs across America. These had been followed by the *Funny Girl* soundtrack and the aforementioned *A Happening In Central Park*, and 1969 would bring *What About Today?*, a not quite successful excursion into the uncharted world of rock and pop.

On 2 July 1969, Barbra was the first artiste to take to the stage of the Las Vegas Hilton, the newly constructed $60 million hotel and casino complex which should have been opened by Elvis Presley – his Svengali, 'Colonel' Tom Parker, had advised him against this, declaring that someone else might be better experiencing the establishment's potential teething problems. Barbra was paid $400,000 for her four-week stint, but allegedly as much again in hotel stock when the management were told of the tremendous stagefright which had plagued her since the Central Park fiasco. Her first night bombed: because the workmen had still been in the auditorium when she had turned up for rehearsals – the foreman had insisted on her wearing a hard hat – she eschewed the sumptuous gown she had planned and walked on to the stage wearing denim overalls and a check shirt as the orchestra struck up the introduction to her first song, 'I Got Plenty Of Nothing'.

The largely celebrity audience were horrified, even more so when Barbra sang several more numbers before speaking to them. They and the attendant press thought she was taking them for a ride, and this was reflected in the sparse applause which greeted each item in her 80-minute set. Worse still, her mostly Yiddish-inspired jokes were met with a glacial silence.

The next evening, Barbra changed tactics. Dressed superbly, she opened with 'Don't Rain On My Parade', the boisterous turn-of-the-century street scene anthem from *Hello, Dolly!*, and earned thunderous applause for this and every song, along with a ten-minute standing ovation at the close. Her final performance was memorable too in that Elvis Presley – scheduled to follow her with his own season now that she had 'tested the water' – was sitting in the audience.

After her film liaison with Montand, which some critics, having seen the rushes, predicted would flop, Barbra's producer friend, Ray Stark, advised her to stick with what she was best at – zany, offbeat comedy with a hint of pathos. Around this time, she co-founded with Sidney Poitier and Paul Newman First Artists, an independent production company that would have complete control over scripts, directors and co-stars. Later the outfit would be augmented by Dustin Hoffman and Steve McQueen. Again she chose an ex-Broadway play, this time Bill Manhoff's *The Owl And The Pussycat*, which had starred Diana Sands and Alan Alda.

In her first adult-themed movie, billed as 'a tale of sexual passion', Barbra played good-hearted hooker Doris Wilgus who falls for aspiring author Felix Sherman (George Segal). One scene called for her to appear topless, but was later cut upon her insistence – Barbra demanded that the negative also be destroyed, which of course did not happen, and it subsequently joined the bootleggers' roster along with similar material of Marilyn Monroe, Garbo and Joan Crawford. The repartee between Streisand the natural wit, and Segal, who had not done comedy before, was electric. Felix 'demotes' himself by pretending to be a bookstore clerk; Doris tells him she is an actress who once appeared in a film – *Cycle Sluts*. She also curses like a sailor on shore leave – in one scene thought to have contained the first on-screen expletive uttered by a major Hollywood star (cut in some prints) she politely says to a group of pestering hoodlums, 'I beg your pardon, boys, but you're intruding on my privacy and I would appreciate it very much – if you don't mind – if you would just *fuck off!*' The film was a huge hit, grossing over $30 million at the US box office. Hot on the heels of her triumphs in *Funny Girl* and *Hello, Dolly!*, this enabled Barbra's name to enter the *Top Ten Box Office Attractions* list for the first time. As her biographer James Spada observed, 'She had made the transformation from dinosaur Dolly to dirty-mouthed Doris, and for Barbra there would be no looking back.'

As the 1970s dawned, Barbra could be seen on the arm of a new paramour – Canadian premier Pierre Trudeau, over twenty years her senior. The pair attended a gala celebrating Manitoba's centenary in January 1970, and their affair caused such consternation – Trudeau was unmarried, and a Catholic – that he was actually asked by a television chat-show host how serious the relationship was, in view of the fact that his response would be of national importance. Barbra, for her part, was asked if she would consider giving up her career to become Canada's First Lady, but whereas Trudeau told his interviewer to mind their own business, Streisand was apparently intrigued by the idea. What she did not know was that Trudeau was seeing someone else – the even younger Margaret Sinclair would become Mrs Trudeau in March 1971.

For a little while, having completed four major films, seven studio albums, a long-running show and scores of television and concert appearances in less than three years, Barbra tried to rest and spend some more time with son Jason. She bought a sumptuous new home in Carolwood Drive, Beverly Hills, and for a few months owned an expensive Art Deco town house in New York's East 80th Street. But the lure of the microphone proved too hard to resist for long and during the summer she began working on *The Singer*, a collection of ballads composed mostly by the French composer Michel Legrand – though the title track, Streisand's homage to Edith Piaf, came from the pen of Walter Marks. This was subsequently aborted in favour of the more contemporary *Stoney End*, which contained cover versions of songs by more contemporary scribes Laura Nyro, Randy Newman, Harry Nilsson and Joni Mitchell – and *Barbra*

Joan Streisand, more tuneful with works by John Lennon, Burt Bacharach and Legrand. Both would sell well, though not in the same massive quantities as the 'regular' Streisand albums.

Early in 1971, Barbra began negotiating a contract with Peter Bogdanovich which seems to have come about after the director had engaged Elliott Gould for his *A Glimpse Of Tiger*, with Kim Darby. Gould had subsequently dropped out of the picture, claiming that he was suffering from nervous exhaustion, and Bogdanovich, not wishing to miss out on the publicity (Gould and Barbra were still married) offered Gould's part to Ryan O'Neal and Darby's to Barbra, who had been dating the blond, hunky *Love Story* star for several weeks. Neither was interested in the script, but both were passionate about working with Bogdanovich, having been hugely impressed by his *The Last Picture Show*.

It did not take Bogdanovich long to come up with the perfect vehicle – *What's Up Doc?* It was a screwball comedy in the same vein as the Cary Grant–Katharine Hepburn classics of the 1930s, but with all the risqué elements employed in those made by Doris Day and Rock Hudson three decades later. Barbra played Judy Maxwell, a bright but bungling young thing who falls for musicologist Howard Bannister, who has developed a theory about primeval man's musical affinity with igneous rocks – not far removed from Grant's fossil scientist character in his and Hepburn's *Bringing Up Baby*. The highlight of the production is a hilarious car chase: pursued by gangsters through the streets of San Francisco, Judy and Howard plough through a huge plate glass window, down several hundred steep stone steps, in and out of a Chinese New Year dragon, through cement, and eventually into the bay. *What's Up, Doc?* premiered at New York's Radio City Music Hall on 9 March 1972 – by which time Barbra had ended her relationship with O'Neal – and proved her biggest draw to date, grossing over $70 million at the box office.

In stark contrast, Barbra's next film barely recovered its

25

production costs. *Up The Sandbox* was her debut production for First Artists. In it she played Margaret Reynolds, a New York housewife with two children and a doting college professor husband (David Selby) who unexpectedly finds herself pregnant again and, weary of the rut she thinks she is in, imagines herself in a series of fantastical scenarios: joining a black revolutionary group to blow up the Statue of Liberty, exposing Fidel Castro – literally – as a woman with huge breasts, being rescued from a wacky abortion clinic, and being attacked by an angry tribe of African warriors – the later taking up ten minutes of screen time but necessitating a four-week location shoot in Nairobi.

The film, though nowhere near as funny as *What's Up, Doc?*, certainly did not deserve the panning it received from the critics – the hugely influential *Variety* leading the assault, dismissing it as 'an untidy melange of overproduced, heavy-handed fantasy' – though such barbed comments arguably had less to do with Barbra and Selby's performances than with the film's feminist issues. As Pauline Kael reported in her *New Yorker* column, 'She's a complete reason for seeing a movie, as Garbo was.'

Desperate for a blockbuster hit, in the spring of 1973 Barbra turned to former mentor Ray Stark, and in an unprecedented volte-face he cast her opposite Robert Redford, her most charismatic co-star since Yves Montand, in the sugary, semi-serious comedy, *The Way We Were*. She played Jewish political activist Katie Morosky who becomes infatuated with and eventually marries WASP jock and wannabe writer Hubbell Gardiner (Redford).

Beginning in the late 1930s and progressing to the Communist witch hunt of the 1950s, the story tells of how Katie actively and vociferously supports the Communist movement, believing that it holds the key to world peace – simultaneously pushing the indolent Hubbell towards the literary career of which he dreams. Hubbell writes a brilliant novel, only to have it almost reduced to trash once it is turned into a Hollywood film. Then his and Katie's marriage disintegrates as she becomes increasingly involved with left-wing politics. They divorce, she marries a Jewish lawyer, and Hubbell becomes a television scriptwriter. At the end of the film, à la *Brief Encounter*, they meet again and reflect on the past.

Securing Redford, whom Barbra had drooled over in the 1966 film of Tennessee Williams' *This Property Is Condemned*, was not an easy task, though this apparently had more to do with Redford's definition of Hubbell being a man totally void of conviction or purpose than his fear of working with the frequently over-demanding Streisand, as has been suggested. Both Ray Stark and director Sidney Pollack, who had made *Property* and Redford's later *Jeremiah Johnson*, hounded him to take the part, and he is said to have capitulated only when offered $1.2 million – more than Columbia were paying Barbra.

Shooting began in the middle of September at Schenectady Union College, New York, moved to Hollywood one month later, and wound up early in December. There were more on-set problems than on her last few films: the cameraman was Harry Stradling Jr, the son of Barbra's favourite cinematographer who had recently died, and the young man was extremely pedantic in his efforts to film her in exactly the right light, taking much longer to get the angles than his father would have done, much to her co-star's annoyance. There was also some antagonism between Stark and Redford, who was quoted as saying that making the film had been 'like doing overtime at Dachau'. Redford is also said to have been paranoid about his sex scene with Barbra, early in the film – this takes place when he is drunk and she takes advantage of the situation by slipping into his bed. Hubbell wakes for a moment, rapidly makes love to her, then immediately falls asleep on top of her. For what should have been a single take, for modesty's sake Redford had put on two jockstraps, but Harry Stradling Jr had asked him to remove these because they had been visible through the flimsy sheet. According to James Spada, 'The look of ecstasy on Barbra's face in the scene likely reflected reacting more than acting.'

The Way We Were, with its superb score by Marvin Hamlisch, premiered in October 1973, yet despite its success (it grossed over $50 million) some critics were again disparaging. Though most generally favoured Barbra's input – *Newsday* called her 'the foremost movie actress of her generation' – many declared that Robert Redford, still at his peak as Hollywood's 'Golden Boy', simply had not been given enough to do in the film, and that its advertised theme – communism – was far too muted. In fact, this and Redford's part had fallen victim to the cutting room in such a way that Arthur Laurents, upon whose novel the script was based and who himself had been interrogated by the Un-American Activities Committee at the start of the McCarthy witch hunt, refused to acknowledge that he had ever been involved with the project. Barbra herself is also said to have been incensed by the removal of her favourite scene – the one where she wears a Gloria Swanson-style turban – though there was small consolation when Columbia allowed her to use one of the stills on the sleeve of the album soundtrack.

Barbra's next venture, *For Pete's Sake*, initially seemed very promising because it had been co-scripted by Stanley Shapiro, who had devised *Pillow Talk* for Rock Hudson and Doris Day – and who would very much have preferred Hudson to have appeared in this one, had he not been deeply involved with his *McMillan And Wife* television series. As such, Barbra was teamed up with the amenable but less engaging Michael Sarrazin for this unlikely tale of a couple who invest in pork bellies on the stock exchange with money the wife has borrowed from the Mafia. When the bottom unexpectedly falls out of the market, they are menaced by the Mob. To regain the money Streisand's character becomes a part-time whore while her husband is out at work, then a courier for a crime cartel, and finally a cattle-rustler, where in the second most hilarious moment in a Streisand movie (after *What's Up, Doc?*) she ends up astride a Brahma bull which goes on the rampage through the San Francisco streets before finally crashing into...a china shop.

Released in 1974, the critics tended to dismiss *For Pete's Sake* as a big-budget B-movie. It performed moderately at the box office, despite being an extremely funny, well put together piece of slapstick. Oh well, no accounting for taste. On the personal front, though, it brought an unexpected dividend in the form of Jon Peters, the lover who would last longer than most.

At twenty-eight – three years her junior – Peters had become interested in Barbra when she asked him to design a wig for her character in the film, a job which, as millionaire hairdresser to the stars and social set, he had considered beneath him. According to the story, he had been summoned to the Carolwood Drive house and she had kept him waiting for too long – a Streisand trait which annoyed even her closest friends. Peters bawled her out before telling her, 'You've got a great ass!'

Tall, solidly built, dark, bearded and hirsute (mother Italian, father half Cherokee Indian), the loquacious crimper had impressed Barbra with tales of his misspent youth – expelled from several schools, he had mixed with a rough crowd and ended up in a borstal. He had married at fifteen, divorced at nineteen and encouraged by his mother (her family owned Pagano's, the Beverly Hills beauty parlour), he had taken up hairdressing *and* professional boxing. Soon after, he borrowed money to open his first salon in the San Fernando Valley, since which time he had rapidly extended his business interests and not looked back.

In 1967 Peters had married again – to actress Lesley Anne Warren, Elliott Gould's co-star in *Drat! The Cat!*, a union which had produced a son, Christopher. Most of all, Barbra was impressed by their 'common links': the fact that the man she often referred to as her soulmate had also lost his father when very young and had been subject to a bullying stepfather – and found it necessary, like herself, to drop a letter from his first name.

The Streisand–Peters relationship would prove as stormy as it was obviously passionate. Peters was reputed to have been one of the few people who dared stand up to her, something she respected, but he had an unpredictable temper and his violent streak was well-publicised at the time. Lesley Anne Warren took out a restraining order against him and he was said to have had a nasty altercation with Elliott Gould over the latter's visitation rights to Jason. In December 1974 the newspapers reported an attack on a car salesman who had made disparaging remarks about Barbra's looks which had left the man so badly injured that he had been declared unfit to ever work again. The relationship also brought out several very open admissions about Barbra's sex life. She would tell *Playboy* in 1977 how with Peters she had become 'sexually aggressive', how they watched pornographic films together – but fell asleep during *Deep Throat* – and how she owned 'some erotic art books'. Speaking to the same magazine the following year, Peters would be more forthright, declaring, 'Good in bed means giving head.'

The couple decided to live together, at least independently in the same estate complex, during the spring of 1974 when between them they purchased eight acres of land in Ramirez Canyon, Malibu, where they built separate houses. Over the next two years, following Peters' divorce from his wife, they would buy up another fifteen neighbouring acres, Barbra would sell the house on Carolwood Drive and Peters would relinquish his salons to devote more time to producing her projects.

Blinded by love, Barbra had to fight with the Columbia Records executives – who rightly accused Peters of having absolutely no experience with such things – to take on *Butterfly*, the concept album slated by the critics as the worst

Barbra had ever made (despite the fact that it went gold within twelve weeks of its October 1974 release) and who lampooned its cover photographs of a 'butterfly' (i.e., a fly on a block of butter) and the explicit lyrics referring to 'Guava Jelly', a seemingly unabashed allusion to semen and a woman's belly which has Barbra breathlessly pleading, 'Rub it, rub it!' Fortunately, perhaps, *Butterfly* was the first and last album Jon Peters produced.

Initially, Barbra was firmly against Ray Stark's final contractual obligation with her – *Funny Lady*, the sequel to *Funny Girl* which, bypassing much of the tense drama over her latter years, covers Fanny Brice's story from her acrimonious divorce from Nick Arnstein to her loveless marriage to songwriter-producer Billy Rose, who pushed her infamous 'Baby Snooks' radio broadcasts, a role she reprised for a cameo appearance in an early Judy Garland film.

When she read Jay Presson Allen's script, however – he of *Cabaret* fame – Barbra soon changed her mind and shooting began on 1 April 1974. Herbert Ross was again brought in to direct the entire production, including the musical tableaux, and, following a disagreement between Ross and the cameraman Vilmos Zsigmond, veteran James Wong Howe was brought in at the last minute. Seventy-six and in poor health, Howe had not worked on a musical since *Yankee Doodle Dandy* in 1941, and would die the next year. Barbra's and everyone else's biggest worry was who should play Billy Rose, a short (4 feet 11 inches), squat and unattractive man, the latter physically and personally. However, the Hollywood dream machine intervened again and simply reinvented Rose in the lofty, handsome form of James Caan, one of Al Pacino's co-stars in *The Godfather*. Omar Sharif, older and a little greyer, was re-engaged to play Arnstein.

Previewed early in 1975, many critics found *Funny Lady* better and more entertaining than its predecessor, doubtless because some of them were still reeling from the 'schlock horror', as one critic put it, of *For Pete's Sake*. It was not: for one thing, there were no songs of the 'People'/'My Man' calibre, no roisterous 'Don't Rain On My Parade'-style anthem.

With another tremendous success tucked under her belt, against the better judgement of her peers – coerced into the project by self-styled guru Jon Peters – Barbra opted to cast caution to the winds by announcing a First Artists–Barwood remake of *A Star Is Born*. First filmed in 1937 as a non-musical with Janet Gaynor and Frederic March, and definitively in 1954 with Judy Garland as the star on her way up and James Mason as her alcoholic has-been of a husband, Barbra knew that such an enterprise was tantamount to courting box office suicide, particularly when it was revealed that the co-star was to be the singer Kris Kristofferson (after Elvis Presley had been 'auditioned' and allegedly rejected for 'being over the hill'). Kristofferson was an actor whose on-screen charisma, compared with that of James Mason, was virtually non-existent. To further complicate matters, the inexperienced, ubiquitous Jon Peters would produce.

Peters hired a director, Frank Pierson, almost as green as himself. Though renowned as a scriptwriter, Pierson had made just one unsuccessful feature film, *The Looking Glass War* in 1969. On the positive side, it was he who brought in three-time Oscar-winning cameraman Robert Surtees, who had excelled with *Ben Hur* in 1959. It came as no surprise when the press, without even waiting to see how the project turned out, dubbed it 'Hollywood's Biggest Joke'. Worse still, on 24 January 1975 a feature appeared in *New Times* magazine not just ridiculing the couple but, alluding to Peters' previous profession, also including a doctored photograph of a bald-headed Streisand. The caption read, 'A STAR IS SHORN: A Beverly Hills Hairdresser Started with Barbra Streisand's Head – Now He Is Taking Over Her Image, Her Career And Her Newest Movie!'

In fact, Kristofferson's dullness and earthiness of character played off against Barbra's vibrancy and tenderness, not to mention arguably one of the best musical scores of the decade. It served to make it her best film since *Hello, Dolly!*, and her most successful so far, its switch from torch singing to frequently tuneless stadium rock and emotional-sexual content bearing little resemblance to the Garland–Mason classic apart from the inevitably sad, tragic ending. In Barbra's opinion, both Gaynor and Garland had portrayed passive women, in keeping with the times, but this was the 1970s, where wives and girlfriends no longer just sat around and watched helplessly whilst their men held their finger on the self-destruct button – they helped! *This* woman, too, was the one taking the role-reversal initiative in the film's love scenes – painting her lover's face with glitter and make-up whilst he made her a beard of soapsuds, climbing on top of *him* in bed and taking off her own clothes first, running the tub and surrounding it with lighted candles the way she did for Peters at home.

Shooting, however, was extremely traumatic. Barbra and Kristofferson did not get along at all. Almost a carbon copy of John Norman Howard, his rock-star alter ego in the film, Kristofferson drank heavily on the set and went through what he described as 'massive quantities of laughin' tobacco'. One of their bust-ups, peppered with expletives, was broadcast publicly at Phoenix's Sun Devil Stadium (the location for the concert scenes) when a technician forgot to switch off the soundstage microphones. An astonished crowd of onlookers and press were entertained by Kristofferson telling Jon Peters exactly what he thought about *his* contribution to the picture. Having already told the star to 'fuck herself', he now roared, 'I ain't trusting my career to no Vegas singer and her hairdresser. If I want shit out of you I'll squeeze your head!'

Barbra's leading man was not the only one to air his grievances in public and declare that he would never work with her and Peters again. Paul Williams, who wrote the score, later told the press 'Working with Streisand and Peters was like having a picnic at the end of an airport runway'. Frank Pierson went a step further, preparing a forty-page dossier which he had printed and circulated to most of the major magazines. *My Battles With Barbra And Jon* ended up, albeit vastly trimmed, gracing the cover of *New West*. To Barbra's way of thinking, perhaps, such insults, though deeply unnerving, were unimportant. By sheer will power and belief in her abilities, she had transformed a 'dubious foible' into a beyond-her-wildest-dreams triumph which grossed $10 million within one week of its Christmas 1976 release, and which with international sales topping the $150 million mark, was one of the most financially successful musicals of the 20th century. On top of this, the soundtrack album sold five million copies and the single 'Evergreen' – for which Barbra wrote the music, in every sense a *chanson-réaliste* which remains one of her best movie songs – topped the American chart and others around the world. Like 'People' and 'Why Did I Choose You?', it remains essentially a Streisand property song which no one else may sing without fear of offending her fans.

A Star Is Born elevated Barbra to Number Two in the *Top Ten Box Office List*. The film won five Golden Globes (Best Actress, Actor, Score, Film, Song) and at the Academy Awards 'Evergreen' won for Barbra and Paul Williams the Oscar for Best Original Song of 1976. And, of course, the enormity of all this left Barbra in a quandary. *What would she do to follow this?* It would take her another three years to come up with the answer.

Meanwhile, between 'doing up' her Malibu complex, Barbra made numerous visits to the recording studio. *Lazy Afternoon*, titled courtesy of the song introduced by Marlene Dietrich in her 1950s cabaret act, was co-produced by singer-songwriter Rupert Holmes – she had hired the young man to score *A Star Is Born*, only to have him walk off the set after an altercation with Jon Peters. The deferred *Classical Barbra*, recorded in May 1973 but not released until early 1976 on account of her deliberating over whether she should release an album so vastly different than anything she had done before, ultimately proved that she could sing absolutely anything. Her interpretation of Canteloube's *Chanson de l'Auvergne*, 'Brezairola', compares easily with that of Victoria de los Angeles. At the opposite end of the spectrum there was *Streisand Superman* in 1977 and *Songbird* from May 1978 which contained her stunning solo reading of Neil Diamond's 'You Don't Bring Me Flowers'.

As with *What's Up, Doc?*, Barbra's next film project came about as the result of a first refusal. *Knockout*, set in the spit and sawdust world of boxing, had been originally scripted for James Caan, who was to have shared top billing with Diana Ross. But when Caan dropped out and Warner Brothers approached, among others, Ryan O'Neal, he insisted that if he did the film, it would only be with Streisand. She accepted the project (her final commitment to First Artists, which would soon be wound up) only on the proviso that boxing expert Jon Peters would produce – which brought no objections from the studio, considering his contribution to the staggering success of his first film, though the presence of a current and former lover on the set at the same time would almost certainly guarantee more than a few fireworks. Howard Zieff was brought in to direct – but after the Frank Pierson press episode, a clause was added to his contract which prohibited him from speaking ill of Barbra or Peters for the rest of his life. A budget of $7 million was agreed, the title was changed to *The Main Event*, and shooting began in October 1978.

In this hilarious battle-of-the-sexes comedy, Barbra played Hilary Kramer, the boss of Le Nez (The Nose) perfume company whose business manager runs off with all her money, leaving her with a single asset – Eddie 'Kid Natural' Scanlon (O'Neal), an ex-boxer now working as a driving instructor whom the manager had acquired as a shady tax write-off. Hilary convinces Scanlon to return to the ring and make her some money – and of course, they fall in love.

The film premiered on 22 June 1979 – Barbra sadly observing that this was the tenth anniversary of Judy Garland's death. The publicity posters, considered raunchy at the time, featured a mock sparring shot with a gloved, sexy-looking, bra-less Barbra in vest and skimpy satin shorts, 'squaring up' to a bare-chested O'Neal, profile to profile. Financially, the production was triumphant, grossing over $80 million. It was her most successful film after *A Star Is Born* and *What's Up, Doc?* but it received such a critical battering that any hope of Barbra completing a movie trilogy with Ryan O'Neal, as had happened with the Hudson-Day partnership, was soon scuppered. Indeed, this time the hacks went too far in their personal attacks on the star, *Motion Picture* especially, which declared, 'It's a shame the male lead was prettier that the female, but that's usually the case with Streisand'.

Streisand enthusiasts – and quite a few detractors – tended to think of *The Main Event* as 'the Barbra butt' movie on account of cameraman Mario Tosi's predilection to home in as much as possible on her not unattractive *derrière* – also a prominent feature on the cover of the *Streisand Superman* album. 'This star seems to labour under the delusion that it is not so much her face as her bottom that is her fortune,' Richard Schikel observed in *Time* magazine, adding, 'It's not a *bad* bottom, but you can't really make a movie of it.' Ernest W. Cunningham cracked in his massively entertaining 1998 *Ultimate Barbra* trivia book, 'Despite the critical acclaim, her butt was not given a screen credit: Barbra may not have wanted to pay its union dues.'

Spending so much time working and living together had started to take its toll on the Streisand–Peters relationship, and toward the end of 1979 the press began speculating that it was all but over. Peters may not have helped to quell the unsettled waters by confiding to *Newsday*, 'We fight and war and battle. Sometimes she is totally crazy.' For a while the seemingly inevitable parting of the ways was stemmed by a series of psychiatric therapy sessions, not just for the couple but for their sons. Barbra is said to have been hurt by Peters' apparent unwillingness to attend her son's bar mitzvah on 5 January 1980, though by this time their affair seems to have been beyond redemption. Peters had moved out of the Malibu complex, and Barbra had temporarily relocated to New York.

The Main Event and its aftermath gave way to another two years of celluloid inactivity. Her next film venture, however, would somewhat sour her already shaky reputation for money-grabbing – though it has to be said that Hollywood studios only paid the huge fees she demanded because they were confident that they would get good returns.

All Night Long began shooting during the spring of 1980 as a low budget picture with tough guy actor Gene Hackman playing George Dupler, who in the throes of midlife crisis flings a chair through his boss's window and gets demoted to running an overnight drugstore. Here, he meets wacky Cheryl Gibbons, his punch-drunk son's insufferably giddy Marilyn Monroe-clone married girlfriend. The promotional poster, supposed to be funny but succeeding only in looking tacky, depicted Cheryl sliding down a fireman's pole, her skirt billowing above her waist and revealing her panties, while George, his son and Cheryl's husband are gazing on her from below. Underneath was an even tackier caption: 'She has a way with men and she's getting away with it – *all night long!*'

Shooting was well under way when the director, Jean-Claude Tramont, sensationally fired Hackman's leading lady, Lisa Eichhorn (the star of the 1979 film, *Yanks*), allegedly for not being funny enough. Her being replaced by Barbra might have gone unnoticed, certainly without attracting the publicity it did, had it not been for her inordinate salary demand – $4 million, plus fifteen per cent of the profits, which resulted in the press dubbing Cheryl Gibbons 'the most expensive supporting role in movie history' – whereas Eichhorn had only been paid $250,000. What made matters worse was that Tramont's wife,

Sue Mengers, was at that time Barbra's agent, so it was inevitable that the director was suspected not just of favouritism, but of engineering the entire situation for financial gain. True or not, taking Barbra on board doubled the film's budget and many declared that its subsequent failure at the box office (equalling *Up The Sandbox* as Barbra's lowest grosser) was inadvertent justice for the ordeal Lisa Eichhorn had been put through.

After the *All Night Long* debacle, Barbra swore that she would never work under another director again – with one exception, she has been good to her word. In 1969 she had purchased the screen rights to Isaac Bashevis Singer's short story, *Yentl, The Yeshiva Boy*, which tells the story of a young Polish woman who in 1904, after the death of her father, is compelled to disguise herself as a boy in order to learn the *Torah*, the first five books of the Hebrew Bible (Christian Old Testament) which are ascribed to Moses. On first examination, the idea of using such a story for a Streisand film seems implausible, particularly as it calls for Yentl to fall in love with a woman, Hadass (Amy Irving) who is prohibited from marrying her fiancé, Avigdor (Mandy Patinkin) because his brother has committed suicide. Effectively, so that Avigdor and Hadass may remain intimate, the latter 'weds' Yentl without realising that 'he' is a she.

For several years, Barbra had hawked the project around the major Hollywood studios, and all had turned it down, declaring the content had been too ethnic. She herself had co-written the script with British actress Maureen Lipman's husband, Jack Rosenthal, whose *The Bar Mitzvah Boy* she had raved about, and she had conducted a lengthy search for the ideal Avigdor. Richard Gere had come close to signing the contract, but had allegedly been dropped because he had expressed disapproval at being directed by Streisand. Barbra's second choice had been French-Algerian *chanteur* Enrico Macias, whose Israeli-Egyptian reconciliation songs had moved her during a trip to

Paris. She had eventually chosen Mandy Patinkin, who had played Che Guevara in the Broadway production of *Evita* and scored a hit in the film *Ragtime* – later he would feature in the television series *Chicago Hope*. It was only when Barbra announced that she was planning to turn *Yentl* into a musical that the studio bosses showed any great interest in the work – with all the songs to be performed by herself, much to Patinkin's annoyance – and at the beginning of 1982 *Yentl* was accepted by United Artists and assigned a budget of $14 million.

There were, however, certain conditions. Barbra would have to accept no more than $3 million for acting, a Director's Guild minimum salary of $80,000, and if she exceeded the budget she would have to give up control over the film. This she apparently agreed to without much of a fight. James Spada quotes her as having said, 'I had to eat shit...Nothing mattered to me except getting this movie made'.

As the twenty-eight-year-old gender-bending Yentl, forty-year-old Barbra fulfils her dream and gives a warm, sensitive, ultimately convincing performance – without any doubt her finest dramatic role, even if so as not to offend morally minded sponsors and some religious groups (particularly as there is a scene where Yentl and Hadass kiss) the advertising campaign included the slogan, 'In a time when the world of study belonged only to men, there lived a girl who dared ask – "*Why?*"'

Yentl is beautifully filmed. During pre-production Barbra travelled to Prague in search of a turn-of-the-century location, then to Amsterdam, where she spent some time in the Rembrandt Museum. Later she hired David Watkin, the cameraman from *Chariots Of Fire*, to transfer images from some of the museum's legendary canvases on to the big screen. The location shooting took place in Roztyly, a small town in Czechoslovakia, between July and October 1982. The conditions, particularly the weather and sanitation, were atrocious, but there were few reported problems. The film was quickly edited in order for the finished print to be available before the Oscar nominations closed. It premiered on 16 November 1983 and attracted some of Barbra's best ever reviews. Even the frequently condemnatory *Newsweek* enthused, 'It's rare to see such a labour of love – Director Streisand has given Star Streisand her best vehicle since *Funny Girl*.' *Time*, equally feisty in the past, now declared, 'Streisand has gone for the emotional goods to create a sweeping musical drama out of a tiny romantic triangle – and, miracle of miracles, she has delivered them!' One of the handful of detractors was Isaac Bashevis Singer himself, who disapproved of Barbra's 'hogging' of the film, even in scenes where Yentl was not on the screen, and for turning his creation into a singer. In a somewhat condescending self-interview for the *New York Times* in January 1984, Singer scathed, 'The leading actress must make room for others to have their say and exhibit their talents. No matter *how* good you are, you don't take everything for yourself.'

The film took over $50 million at the US box office, even more overseas. Barbra became the first woman to win a Golden Globe, but the much hoped-for Oscar evaded her, it is widely believed because of the sexist attitude of some Academy sponsors – the only winner was Michel Legrand, for the score.

Perhaps in an attempt to salvage what was left of their strained relationship, Jon Peters had visited the *Yentl* set in Europe. If this was the case, he had wasted his time, for there was now a new man in Barbra's life – ice-cream heir and sometime country music composer Richard Baskin, who was very quickly put to work in the recording studio.

Barbra's 1980 album, *Guilty*, part-produced and written by the Bee Gees' Barry Gibb, though by no means her most electric and melodious, had proved her biggest ever money-spinner, her fifth to top the *Billboard* chart, selling twenty million copies worldwide and with three of its extracted singles hitting the Top Ten. *Memories*, which had followed at the end of 1981, though artistically superior, had been more or less a greatest hits anthology – containing just two new songs, one of these Andrew Lloyd Webber's 'Memory' from *Cats*, which Barbra had recorded in London.

After this had come the *Yentl* soundtrack. Richard Baskin was just one of nine producers, including Barbra herself, who dabbled in *Emotion*, recorded in thirteen different studios – and it shows. The songs and arrangements are not up to Barbra's characteristically impeccable standards, and the album barely scraped into the *Billboard* Top Twenty. The *San Francisco Chronicle's* Joel Selvin was probably reflecting the opinions of thousands of bemused and disappointed fans when he wrote, 'There are people out there who actually respect Streisand as an artist – but this could cure them.'

Barbra and thirty-three-year-old Baskin – an imposing figure, 6 feet 4 inches tall with a shock of dark, curly hair – began dating publicly in February 1984. Around the same time, Jon Peters sold her his share of the Malibu complex, a move which also signalled a return to the fold for Marty Erlichman, who had stopped being Barbra's agent in 1978 when Peters had 'started running the show'. During a recent trip to Europe to promote *Yentl*, Barbra had told journalists that, now they were no longer an item, she and Peters had a much better understanding and respect for one another. 'People who live together can't help taking each other for granted,' *Paris Match* quoted her as saying, 'they only end up hating themselves. I won't be making that mistake again.' Even so, after a short time her new beau had moved in with her, and gossip columnists began speculating that wedding bells might be ringing in the not too distant future.

During the summer of 1985, Richard Baskin was close at hand for Barbra's next series of sojourns in the recording studio. *The Broadway Album*, for which she was reunited with old pal Peter Matz, certainly proved that lessons had been learned from past mistakes. Without any doubt, for sheer professionalism, choice of material, musical arrangements and vocality *par excellence*, this was Barbra's best original studio album for more than a decade. 'It was time for me to do something I truly believed in,' she later recalled, and *The Broadway Album* rocketed to the top of the charts.

The album's staggering success resulted in Barbra being inundated with concert engagements, and both her management and Columbia urged her to tour. Some press reports suggested that in persistently refusing to do so, she was punishing her fans, who had elevated her to the privileged position as America's top singing star after Frank Sinatra. She was, of course, terrified of facing audiences and had been since the Central Park episode. Since appearing at *The Stars Salute Israel At 30* in May 1978, she had made only one live appearance, in June 1980, when she had performed several songs with Michel Legrand at an American Civil Liberties fundraiser honouring her songwriter friends Alan and Marilyn Bergman.

Barbra's fears, however, were pushed to the back of her mind in the wake of the Chernobyl nuclear disaster of April 1986. Convinced that President Reagan's Republican pro-armament policies were at least partly responsible for there being so many nuclear power plants strategically positioned around the world, she subsequently formed the Streisand Foundation, an organisation aimed at raising funds which would hopefully go towards ousting Reagan and returning the anti-armament Democrats to power. Barbra's fans may have initially been thrilled that she would be taking to the concert platform once more, though this turned to bitter disappointment when it was announced that there would be a single dinner recital for a crowd of just four hundred at her Malibu complex, and with tickets costing a whopping $5,000 a pair. The event took place on 6 September and raised over $1.5 million, three times the amount raised by Reagan at a Republican fundraiser the following evening. Robin Williams was the master of ceremonies, and Barbra sang thirteen songs (including two duets with Barry

Gibb which most people thought out of place), for an exclusively show business audience – all of them fellow Democrats and most of them millionaires.

Barbra's next film was *Nuts*, boldly based on Tom Toper's hugely controversial Broadway play with its central themes of murder, insanity, prostitution and incest. The role of Claudia Draper, the top-class hooker who kills a violent client in self-defence, had been set aside for Bette Midler, Barbra's nearest contemporary, and should have been filmed a few years earlier. Following the failure of The Divine Miss M's inappropriately-titled *Jinxed*, the part had gone to Debra Winger – who in the Hollywood tradition of 'You're only as good as your last film' had been subsequently dropped owing to the poor box-office performance of her *Mike's Murder*. To direct, Universal hired Mark Rydell, who had made *On Golden Pond* and Midler's *The Rose*, and it was he who brought in Barbra – along with a $5 million salary demand as the star, plus an additional $500,000 as producer, her take-it-or-leave-it condition for doing the film. Ironically, Rydell was *himself* ousted from the production when Universal abandoned it and it was taken over by Warner Brothers.

Shooting began in October 1986. The new director was Martin Ritt, whose films *Hud* and *Norma Rae* Barbra had admired, and her co-star – once Dustin Hoffman had apparently been hired and fired for not only demanding equal billing but a bigger salary than Barbra – was Richard Dreyfuss. He plays Aaron Levinsky, the lawyer who tries to convince Claudia's parents and the courts that she is sane, whereas they would rather have her declared mentally unbalanced so that, if found guilty, she will be committed to what they see as the more acceptable environment of an institution rather than be sent to prison. Barbra had seen Dreyfuss in the Los Angeles stage production of Larry Kramer's AIDS drama, *The Normal Heart*, and had even thought about turning this into a film, centring on the US government's, and in particular President

Reagan's, abject indifference towards funding research into a cure for the disease. Maureen Stapleton played her mother and veteran actor Karl Malden was the stepfather who abused her as a child. Playing the murder victim, in a rare heavy role, was comic Leslie Nielsen.

To prime herself for an intensely testing role, Barbra used the Method approach – visiting brothels and psychiatric hospitals, interviewing prostitutes, doctors, schizophrenic patients, legal aid lawyers and suchlike – an experience which so disturbed her that she began making sweeping changes to the script. She also composed the atmospheric score, which is perfectly in keeping with the frequently harrowing storyline. Without any doubt, Claudia Draper remains one of her superlative triumphs of mind over matter and *Nuts* is a credit to Barbra's multifaceted talent.

Sadly, the film was misunderstood and not an immediate success. It was half-heartedly championed by the *Los Angeles Herald Examiner's* Peter Rainer, who quipped, 'A damn sight better that it has any right to be...Whether by edict or design, we get to see Streisand in close-up more often that any actress since Falconetti played Joan of Arc.' The American critics, as opposed to their European counterparts, are always ready to attack an artiste's yearning to stray away from typecasting and made sure that the movie suffered at the box office by mercilessly hammering it into the ground, though by the end of its first season it had managed to recover its production costs.

Barbra's relationship with Richard Baskin had cooled somewhat during the shooting of *Nuts*, though like the deposed Jon Peters, the two would remain good friends. In January 1988, at the Mike Tyson–Larry Holmes world heavyweight championship fight at the Atlantic City Convention Centre, Barbra was spotted holding hands with *Miami Vice* star Don Johnson, and within days the story filled gossip columns in newspapers across America that Streisand had not just found a new man in her life – not just any man, but one of the most virile, sexiest studs in show business. How much of what happened next was actually mere hype, however, is not known. Like most of the others, Johnson would be roped into one of her work projects – *Till I Loved You*, a concept album lacklustre in comparison with her last two, which she declared would chronicle a love affair like a French *chanson*: beginning, middle, end. British singer Dorothy Squires had used the same concept with her *Seasons Of* album, but in the case of Barbra and Johnson the *chanson* would be but brief. His singing in their duet of the title track, quite frankly, is nothing short of awful: as with many of her duets, other than the one with Neil Diamond, her artistry and usual vocal brilliance diminishes because she is performing with artistes who are inferior to herself, and, therefore, has to downgrade emotionally and vocally so as not to 'drown' them.

At thirty-eight, seven years Barbra's junior, Johnson had made a name for himself in the late 1960s playing a male rape victim in Sal Mineo's stage production of the prison drama, *Fortune and Men's Eyes*. Johnson had certainly lived. In 1973, whilst shooting *The Harrad Experiment*, he had fallen for his fourteen-year-old co-star, Melanie Griffith. The pair later married, Johnson's first of three which had ended in divorce by the age of twenty-eight. Prior to playing Sonny Crockett in *Miami Vice*, which ran between 1984 and 1989, his career had been coloured by a much publicised series of battles with drink and drugs, but by the time he met Barbra he had settled down some-what, having enjoyed a lengthy – for him – relationship with Patti D'Arbanville, who had a small part in *The Main Event*.

As with Richard Baskin, many predicted that Barbra and Johnson would tie the knot, particularly when she told reporters, 'Don's the perfect man for me. I'm not going to let him go. He's got it all – looks, brains, personality. He doesn't need anything from me except love.' The pair certainly seemed well matched. Barbra was given a non-speaking cameo role in an episode of *Miami Vice*. For her forty-sixth birthday, in April, Johnson presented her with a ribbon-wrapped Arab stallion which, the press delighted in reporting, had set him back

$25,000, and that the extravagant gesture was his way of asking her to marry him. Around this time a British tabloid revealed how Barbra had declared she would never marry Johnson unless he agreed to be circumcised, not for religious reasons, but for the purpose of hygiene, which cannot have made him feel very comfortable.

There were many, of course, who believed the Streisand-Johnson liaison to have been doomed from the start. He is rumoured to have still been seeing Melanie Griffith, among others, and by the time the *Till I Loved You* album hit the shops at the end of October 1988, Johnson (memorably baptised 'Streisand's Toy Boy Goy' by *Bloom County* cartoonist Berke Breathed) had indeed returned to his ex-wife. The couple would remarry in June 1989, a union which would last only another few years until Griffith became involved with Spanish heart-throb Antonio Banderas.

For her next film, Barbra chose *The Prince Of Tides*, a torrid family melodrama set in South Carolina and based on the novel by Pat Conroy. Told mostly in a series of flashbacks, the story centres around the Wingos – Henry and Lila, their sons Luke and Tom, and Tom's unbalanced twin sister, Savannah. In particular it delves into Tom's mind about his troubled past, and the effect this has not just on him but on those about him. As a boy, he, his mother and sister were raped by escaped convicts, and aided by a pet tiger, he and Luke have murdered the culprits and buried their bodies, but vowed never to tell their father. Now, a generation on, Tom has fallen in love with his sister's therapist, Susan Lowenstein – the role played by Barbra.

Don Johnson had introduced Barbra to Conroy's book, and she had immediately concluded that the screen adaptation would prove the ideal vehicle to properly cement their relationship – changing her mind upon learning that former co-star Robert Redford had bought the screen rights.

For a while it seemed that a reunion might be close at hand – apart from Ryan O'Neal and Omar Sharif, Barbra had never worked twice with the same man, and she was doubtless perturbed by the small talk buzzing around Hollywood circles that 'once with La Streisand was more than enough.' Redford, however, refused to be directed by her and after considering several big names – including Kevin Costner and Tom Berenger – she chose forty-nine-year-old Nick Nolte, a not-so-very-attractive but versatile actor who had collected rave reviews for his part in the television mini-series *Rich Man, Poor Man*. Like many of her co-stars, Nolte had lived a full, hedonistic life, and she believed his experiences would stand him in good stead for his portrayal of Tom Wingo. The supporting roles went to Jeroen Krabbé, Kate Nelligan and Blythe Danner. John Barry was due to compose the score, but after an on-set argument he was replaced by James Newton Howard, Elton John's former keyboard player who had worked on Barbra's *Songbird* and *Emotions* albums, besides scoring the recently released *Pretty Woman*. He and Barbra became lovers, but only for the duration of the film's shooting schedule.

The Prince Of Tides was financed by Columbia Pictures – perhaps surprisingly so, for the executive co-chairman who backed the deal was none other than old flame Jon Peters, who had certainly moved up in the world since their split. Peters sanctioned a $25 million budget, almost one quarter of which went to Barbra.

Barbra's greatest personal joy, however, was that the film allowed her to work with her favourite man – twenty-three-year-old son Jason, who (after Pat Conroy disapproved of her original choice, future *Batman* star Chris O'Donnell) was cast as Bernard, Susan Lowenstein's hot-headed teenage violinist son. Jason was no novice in front of the camera – currently working as a production assistant for Steven Spielberg, he had played several small parts in films (including *Up The Sandbox*) and television dramas, but never anything quite so challenging as this, and under his mother's exacting, hypercritical direction. Like anyone else in the production, Jason was not above getting a dressing down if he made a mistake or stepped out of line.

Some of the on-set altercations between mother and son are said to have been just as vociferous as those with the likes of difficult co-stars such as Kris Kristofferson.

Neither Jason nor Barbra were prepared for the crisis brought about by the headline in the *Star,* one of America's tackiest tabloids, on 15 May 1990, just weeks before *The Prince Of Tides* went into production: 'BARBRA STREISAND HEART-SICK – HER ONLY SON HANGS OUT AT GAY BARS'. Barbra had been aware of Jason's homosexuality, and had readily accepted his decision, two years earlier, to move out of her house and into his own place in the heart of New York's gay area. The way the press handled the matter was unforgivable, particularly when another scandal rag, the *Globe,* printed a follow-up story – only marginally more tasteful than some of the bilge which appeared in the British press – 'BARBRA WEEPS OVER GAY SON'S WEDDING', claiming that Jason had wed his male model lover, David Knight, in a semi-religious ceremony at their home which Barbra had allegedly refused to attend. It was all hogwash, of course, and, rather than sue, Barbra allowed the hacks to have their say – even the insidious individual who announced to the world the incident during the shooting of *The Prince Of Tides* when, in a bustling Central Station, Barbra had yelled to her son, 'Walk like a *man!*'

Eventually, the story would become old news, but it would at least open a new chapter in the Streisand Good Samaritan saga – as a spokeswoman and fundraiser for AIDS charities. In 1997, there would be a coda to this then worrying story when Jason's independently produced film, *Inside Out,* featured at the Sundance Festival. The thirty-minute short film is the story of a young, openly gay son of a famous celebrity whose marriage to a male model, exposed by a 'supermarket tabloid', makes him a subject of ridicule. Barbra's only known public quote regarding the fictitious marriage was when she snapped at a pesky reporter, 'I don't care if my son marries a chimpanzee – I'll be at the wedding!'

At *The Prince Of Tides'* New York premiere on 9 December 1991, Barbra was conspicuous by her absence, though she did attend the gala opening in Los Angeles two evenings later – raising more than a few eyebrows by turning up on the arm of Jon Peters. The critics for once were unanimous that it was a fine film – her best, many thought, since *A Star Is Born*. This was proved, financially at least, when it grossed almost $100,000 at the home box office. In January 1992 the Directors Guild Of America nominated Barbra as Best Director, which was only the third time a woman had walked off with the award, and Women In Film presented her with the Dorothy Arzner Special Recognition Award. The film also received seven Oscar nominations, though *not* for Best Director: the Academy remained, or so it appeared, prejudiced against any woman who dared infiltrate its gung-ho, male dominated tradition. And this was the year, alas, that Jonathan Demme's *The Silence Of The Lambs* swept the board.

On 24 April 1992 Barbra turned 50, and the next day Jon Peters threw a lavish bring-the-family party at his Beverly Hills estate. The press reported how 'Barbra's Magic Castle', complete with circus and fairground attractions, had set him back $200,000. An earlier half-century present had come in the form of *Just For The Record*, a four-album boxed set which traced Barbra's stage, television and recording career all the way back to 1955, when at the age of thirteen she had entered the Nola Recording Studio to sing 'You'll Never Know' to her mother. The collection was not cheap – it cost around $60 – but with over sixty of its ninety-five tracks classified as collectors' rarities it sold well over a million copies. In the February, the Academy of Recording Arts and Sciences presented her with the extremely prestigious Grammy Legend Award. Accepting this from her friend Stephen Sondheim an emotional Barbra told the audience, 'I don't feel like a legend. I feel like a work in progress.'

This particular work in progress was inducted into the Hall

of Fame for Women in Film in June 1992, a platform which she used to attack the presidential regimes of Reagan and Bush for social injustice and across-the-board discrimination, especially against women: 'Not long ago we were referred to as dolls, tomatoes, chicks, babes, broads. We've graduated to being called tough cookies, foxes, bitches, witches. I guess that's progress…A man is commanding, a woman's demanding. A man is forceful, a woman is pushy. A man's uncompromising, a woman's a ball-breaker. A man's a perfectionist, a woman's a pain in the ass…I look forward to a society that is colour- and gender-blind, that judges us by the value of our work, not by the length of our legs.'

With the Democratic presidential nominations imminent, Barbra had pledged her support for Iowa candidate Tom Harkin, but when he dropped out of the preliminaries she plumped for the Governor of Arkansas, Bill Clinton. On 16 September, by which time he had become the party's nominee, Barbra topped the bill at his running mate Al Gore's $1.5 million fundraiser at Beverly Hills. The event was broadcast via satellite to fundraisers across the country. Barbra's thirty-minute set contained songs whose titles befitted the extravaganza: 'It Had To Be You', 'It's A New World', 'Children Will Listen', 'Happy Days Are Here Again'. She told the audience in another impassioned speech: 'I used to be a director, now I've become a backyard singer. The last time I sang live was six years ago to help a Democratic Senate. What motivated me was the disaster at Chernobyl. What motivates me now is another kind of disaster – the possibility of four more years of George Bush and Dan Quayle.'

Barbra began devoting more and more of her time towards her support of the Washington power machine and raising money for several AIDS projects. The press hailed her an FOB – Friend Of Bill – whilst *People* magazine referred to Clinton as an FOB – Friend Of Barbra – emphasising that she was probably the most politically potent of the two. A story also did the rounds of the tabloids, completely unfounded, that she and Clinton had a brief affair. This stemmed from the disclosure that for suitable remuneration, potential campaign donors were allowed to spend a night in the White House's famous Lincoln bedroom. Ernest W. Cunningham observed in *The Ultimate Barbra*, 'Steven Spielberg was said to have contributed $446,023; Chevy Chase, $55,000; Ted Danson, $10,000; and Barbra Streisand $85,000. In Barbra's case, there are rumours that she didn't sleep alone.'

On 19 January 1994, Barbra performed at President Clinton's inaugural gala at the US Air Arena in Landsover, Maryland – by now, some newspapers were dubbing her 'Senator Yentl' and reporting how she was seriously considering running for Democratic Senator of New York. This was untrue, and seems to stem from her having put her Malibu complex on the market, sparking off another rumour that she was thinking of relocating to New York (unable to sell the property for $19 million, later in the year she would donate it to the Santa Monica Mountains Conservancy for a $15 million tax write-off). In the British *Sunday Times* Camille Paglia referred to her as 'America's Second Lady', the *Washington Post* scathingly as 'Hurricane Barbra'. In truth, all she wanted was a president whom she believed would cater for the interests of the so-called underdog and not himself, and now that she had played her part in Clinton's journey to the White House she could return to the more familiar field within which she excelled – entertaining.

First, however, there would be another scandal of sorts – a much-publicised, controversial association with maverick tennis star and acknowledged 'King of Grunge', Andre Agassi. Barbra and Agassi, twenty-eight years her junior and, the press were eager to point out, even younger than her own son, had met shortly after the premiere of *The Prince Of Tides*. He had apparently called her and told her how much the film had moved him. At the subsequent US Open, the television cameras had zoomed in on Barbra, sitting in the VIP box, at every break in the match and pretty much the same thing had happened in June when Agassi faced Pete Sampras at Wimbledon. She told reporters, 'He plays like a Zen master – it's very in the moment!', prompting a good many jibes from critics who had wondered what she had been talking about. Agassi lost the match, and the *Daily Mirror* printed a photograph of an anguished-looking Barbra on its front page with the caption, 'BARBRA CRY-SAND'.

Most American reporters, however, avowed that the Streisand–Agassi romance could only have been platonic because of the latter's no-sex religious convictions. Agassi was also, it was claimed, virulently homophobic (the gay publication, *Village Voice*, reported how, after winning one match he had quipped, 'I'm as happy as a faggot in a submarine'). When Andre Agassi exited her life, most of Barbra's fans must have muttered, given such utterances, 'Good riddance!'

Like all the great divas who had no little difficulty in sustaining marriages and relationships – Piaf, Dietrich, Lenya, Callas, Squires and Garland – Barbra's greatest love had always been with her audiences, that privileged mass which had supported her through good times and bad and never let her down like most of the men in her life. To this end, on 31 December 1993, at the MGM Grand Garden Hotel in Las Vegas, Barbra faced a full-sized audience for the first time in over twenty years.

Her 'saviour' was entrepreneur Kirk Kerkorian, the owner of the Las Vegas Hilton who had engaged her back in 1969 and again in 1972. The 5,000-room Grand Garden, with its 15,000-seater auditorium said to have been the biggest such complex in the world, had cost over $1 billion to build, and for its opening Kerkorian had wanted 'the biggest star in the world'. To persuade her to think about performing for him, Kerkorian gave Barbra $3 million for her to donate to a charity of her choice – two thirds of this was handed over towards research into a cure for AIDS. Then Kerkorian had offered her ninety per cent of the takings, should she decide to perform – an estimated $9 million for two concerts – well aware that the publicity generated by her appearance would still enable him to rake in a healthy profit. Still Barbra deliberated, for no amount of money would have been able to cure her of her almost manic stage fright – if anything, so exorbitant a fee would only make it worse, for fans paying as much as $1,000 for a ticket, probably up to five times this amount once the touts moved in, would expect nothing but the best and pick on even the minutest fault. On top of this they would be 'scalped' by the merchandise stands which had acquired licences to sell T-shirts, gold key rings, suede coats, commemorative postage stamps, crystal glasses – dozens of different items, all at hugely inflated prices to take advantage of what many critics predicted might prove Streisand the singer's swansong.

Finally, she signed the contract and Barbra's friends rallied around to help her prepare for what will now be remembered as the pinnacle of a magnificent career. Copies of the sheet music for every song she had ever sung – almost six hundred – were commissioned so that they could be vetted, whittled down to thirty or so, and suitably arranged with a series of witty monologues to form an autobiographical recital. Earlier in the year, during a trip to Washington and Virginia, she had visited Thomas Jefferson's sumptuous Monticello mansion, and she now asked for its tea-room to be recreated for her stage setting. Asked to choose any orchestra, she plumped for a mega-expensive, sixty-four-piece outfit which would be conducted by Marvin Hamlisch.

Barbra: The Concert (the format of the shows varied but little throughout the tour, the contents of the video being those at Anaheim, 22/24 July 1994) is a unique testimony, equating to Piaf's 1961 Paris Olympia recitals and Garland's Carnegie Hall comeback in the same year. Like them, too, she choose to wear black, traditionally the colour of the *chanteuse-réaliste* who, in taking the audience in the palm of her hand, opens her heart and lays bare her soul – as 'La Streisand' would over the next two hours or so.

A veritable Who's Who of celebrities and politicians filled the first rows of the Grand Garden – relatively unimportant compared with the people who really mattered, the fans who had scrimped and saved and travelled from the four corners of the globe and queued to get in. Barbra also lived up to her legendary tardiness, making her entrance an hour late, by which time excitement in the auditorium had reached fever pitch. Film footage shows her mounting the stage looking very nervous, and when she began her first song – a slightly tremulous 'As If We Never Said Goodbye' which had the audience reacting wildly to almost every line – she clutched the set-rail so tightly that her knuckles turned white. From then on her voice soared from strength to strength, singing not just her own standards but those created by her predecessors – Helen Morgan's 'Can't Help Lovin' That Man', though Barbra's inspiration had come from Ava Gardner's rendition (lip-synching to the voice of Gogi Grant) in the second film version of *Showboat*; Garland's 'The Man That Got Away'; Billie Holiday's 'Lover Man'.

It did not matter that for much of the time Barbra was reading the words from teleprompters (Marlene Dietrich had sometimes done the same), for every syllable she uttered was pure magic. She even managed to poke fun at herself for having submitted to countless hours of therapy – while on the big screen behind her were flashed 'psychiatric' clips from *Nuts, The Prince Of Tides* and *On A Clear Day You Can See Forever* – and to get back to all those who had mispronounced her name in the past, the two imaginary psychoanalysts who 'interviewed' her during her comic monologue did exactly the same. Barbra lusted after Marlon Brando, whom she had first seen in *Guys And Dolls* – he appeared on the screen singing 'I'll Know', and she joined in with him, harmonising beautifully until the image widened to reveal Brando embracing his co-star Jean Simmons, but only for a second before being superimposed by a picture of the teenage Streisand, bringing the exclamation, 'What a *mieskeit!*' And she closed the first half of the show with an 'On A Clear Day' even more superior to the one she had sung in the film with Montand.

The second act was even more intense and thrilling. Dressed in white now, Barbra sang hit after hit as more images flashed on to the screen behind her. She spoke of the meeting with Prince Charles when they had shared a mug of tea. She dedicated a tender 'Not While I'm Around' to Jason, sitting in the audience and looking slightly embarrassed, saying, 'I know he's old enough to take care of himself, but it's always nice to have someone looking out for you no matter how old you are'. She spoke of her greatest celluloid achievement, *Yentl,* performing its most moving songs and duetting with herself on screen, and when she got around to 'Happy Days Are Here Again' she sang this to hardship and oppression images of the Depression, then to the more positive images looking back over Clinton's first year in office.

All too soon it was over, the final curtain before 'Somewhere', now an anthem proclaiming Barbra's aspirations for the world of the future, preceded by a sincere vote of thanks to her fans and an announcement which declared the Streisand credo, the right to individuality: 'Just imagine how boring life would be if we were all the same. My idea of a perfect world is one in which we really appreciate each other's differences. Short, tall. Democrat, Republican. Black, white, gay, straight – a world in which all of us are equal, but *definitely* not the same!'

* * *

In January 1994, Barbra's Carolwood Drive home suffered extensive damage during the 6.7 Richter Scale earthquake which hit the Greater Los Angeles area, killing sixty people and causing millions of dollars worth of damage. Though obviously distressed, once she had recovered from the initial shock Barbra turned a potential tragedy into a charitable money-spinner: lumps of plaster and rubble were sold at a local memorabilia store for $10 each, and in the March over five hundred valuable artworks which she said were no longer of use to her – items which *could* have been damaged, but which were not – were auctioned at Christie's in New York. The sale raised over $5 million, $2 million of which had been paid for a Tamara de Lempicka painting bought by Madonna, who had earlier paid $1 million for Marlene Dietrich's famous 'Busby Berkeley' bracelet. Barbra is reputed to have given most of the money to charity, again most notably to AIDS research.

In the spring of 1994 Barbra 'hit the road' – her first concert tour in twenty-eight years which would take her to London, Washington, Detroit, Anaheim, San Jose and New York. Such was the demand for tickets for her two concerts at London's Wembley Arena on 20 and 27 April that two more were added. The tabloids tried to put a damper on her first professional appearance on British soil since *Funny Girl* in 1966 by declaring that such was her fear of terrorists, she would be performing behind a huge sheet of bullet-proof glass – complete media invention, of course. Then she was criticised for using teleprompters, though when she told her second night audience why she needed these – 'I wouldn't be here if I couldn't use them because I'd never remember the words!' – her honesty was rewarded with yet another standing ovation. *The Times* lauded her 'bravura' performance, whilst the *Daily Mail* called her 'the supreme communicator'.

On 24 April, at London's exclusive Mimmo d'Ischia restaurant with a handful of celebrity pals, Barbra celebrated her fifty-second birthday. Elliott Gould was in town, but had not received an invitation.

The American leg of the tour kicked off with two shows at Washington's US Air Arena on 10 and 12 May, where she had feted Bill Clinton the year before. He and his wife were there again, and on 15, 17 and 19 May she was in Detroit at the

Palace of Auburn Hills, a city which held fond memories, she said, because her season at its Caucus Club in 1961 had represented her first engagement outside New York. By the time she reached Anaheim on 2 June, she was suffering from laryngitis – she managed to battle her way through the show of 4 June, but the remaining four were postponed and tacked on to the end of the tour for mid-July. She was back in fine fettle five days later for two shows at the San Jose Arena, near San Francisco, and on 20 June she opened at New York's famous Madison Square Garden – the seven shows here would rake in over $60 million.

The Streisand wheel of fortune had turned full circle and she was back home where she belonged, receiving so many standing ovations that each evening she left the stage in tears. *The New York Times* ran the headline she had dreamed about as an unhappy, self-professed *mieskeit* kid in Brooklyn, 'LOCAL GIRL MAKES GOOD!'

Before embarking on her 1994 tour, Barbra had become heavily involved in three film projects, each covering a topic close to her heart and relying upon her knowledge of the human condition.

She had taken out an option to produce and star in *The Normal Heart*, Jewish writer and AIDS activist Larry Kramer's acclaimed semi-autobiographical play about the so-called gay plague and the Reagan administration's reluctance to search for a cure, back in 1986. She would portray Dr Emma Brockner, one of the few women in the film and a character secondary to the plot, whose central figures are those unfortunates fighting not just the malady but the virulent prejudices of a bigoted society. Since then, Jason's 'outing' by the press had made Barbra even more determined to make a statement that everyone – gay or straight – had a God-given right to love whomever they chose.

In 1994, the Kramer work, much of it rescripted by Barbra herself, was still waiting to go into production, and Kramer was himself suffering from the virus and terrified of dying before his 'baby' hit the big screen – yet Barbra had opted for directing, producing and starring in a remake of the 1958 French classic, *Le Miroir A Deux Faces*, besides producing *Serving In Silence* for NBC, the true story of Lieutenant-Colonel Margarethe Cammermeyer, the nurse who had been forced to resign from the Washington Station National Guard after twenty-six years for publicly declaring her lesbianism.

Cammermeyer had subsequently hit back at the system, becoming an activist and fighting the American military's out-dated stance prohibiting gays and lesbians from the armed forces. Barbra found the perfect Cammermeyer in Glenn Close, an extremely gifted and sympathetic actress who rarely did television drama. Close was also roped in as co-executive produc-er, and the film was shot on location in Vancouver, with Australian actress Judy Davis portraying Cammermeyer's lover. At once there were problems with potential advertisers – spurred on by a group of New York moralists calling them-selves the Family Defence Council – who threatened to boycott NBC and withdraw their advertising contracts should the two women be seen kissing. Barbra, Close and Davis complained vociferously that if such scenes were cut, the film would lose much of its meaning, and by the time it was broadcast on 6 February 1995, much of the fuss had died down. Though it did not win an award, the mere fact that *Serving In Silence* had been nominated for several Emmys (including Best Actress and Best Film) proved that Barbra had made a sensible decision to film a subject which might go just that little bit further towards ending sexual prejudice.

On 3 February, Barbra gave a lecture at the John F Kennedy School of Government at Harvard University – the topic, *The Artist As Citizen*, proclaiming the rights of show business per-sonalities to publicly air their political beliefs. She had spent the day being escorted around the campus by John F Kennedy Jr and, following in the footsteps of Gore, Gorbachev and other political luminaries, wearing a plain outfit, little make-up and virtually no jewellery, she got over her intense nervousness by asking her student audience, in broadest Brooklynese, 'You heard of *shpilkes*?' What she meant was pins and needles, and the remark had everyone rolling around in hysterics, though by the time she got around to the serious stuff, she was no less captivating than on the concert platform. She denounced the Speaker of the House's request to cut down on government spending by dissolving the Arts budget, arguing that the cost of this equated to just one of the 442 F-22 fighter jets the Pentagon was planning to build which, she emphasised, even military experts had deemed unnecessary. 'One less plane and we've got the whole Arts budget!' she yelled. Then she defended her Hollywood peers: 'Why should the actor give up his role as citizen just because he's in show business? For his role in the movie *Philadelphia*, Tom Hanks had to learn quite a bit about being a gay man with AIDS. Should he have remained silent on this issue? For thirty years Paul Newman has been an outspoken defender of civil liberties and a major philanthropist. Would he be better if he just made money and played golf? Is Robert Redford a bubble-head because he knows more about the environment than most members of Congress?' On and on she went, her confidence growing and her voice gaining momentum, just as would have happened during a concert, hammering home her policies for almost an hour before closing to tumultuous applause and a standing ovation. It is no small wonder, perhaps, that on 21 May another great institution, Brandeis University, would award her an honorary Doctorate of Humane Letters degree for her selfless devotion to those less fortunate than herself.

Also in the spring of 1995, Barbra purchased a new home – a huge mansion in Malibu, built on a bluff known as the Queen's Necklace on account of the way in which its lights sparkled at night-time around the curve of Santa Monica Bay. Later in the year she would buy the two houses next to it, though for a little while longer she would live there without any particular man in her life.

Why Barbra finally relinquished her option on the Kramer work is not clear. It may well be because the author had wanted to include man-to-man sex scenes which she considered too graphic (one reason why Dustin Hoffman refused to appear in it), or maybe because the 'time-bomb' Kramer constantly spoke about, ticking away inside him, made Barbra feel that to rush a project which she once confessed was her most important since *Yentl* – which had taken several years to reach the screen – would compromise her professionalism. Also, she may have felt that the subject of governmental indifference towards AIDS sufferers decidedly 'old-hat' now that there was a more sympathetic administration under her friend, Bill Clinton.

Larry Kramer took rejection badly and was hardly assuaged when Barbra's son Jason, who also happened to be a close friend, offered to step in and produce. Streisand's son, Kramer declared, was 'a sweet kid', but he did not have the experience for a major production. In an interview for *Variety* on 8 April 1996 he publicly denounced her, saying, 'This woman has had this play since 1986. She was all set to make *The Normal Heart* about a worldwide plague, and at the last minute she switches to a film about a woman who gets a facelift. I didn't think that was decent of her to do to me, her gay fans and the people with AIDS she talks so movingly about.'

Barbra was incensed, and hurt, that someone she had looked upon as a friend could have accused her, even in a round about way, of being uncaring, and not unexpectedly she hit back. 'I'm painfully aware of his ticking clock, therefore I'm stepping aside and will be no longer involved with the project,' she told the press, adding for the benefit of would-be detractors, 'I personally have a *strong* commitment to projects that reflect and further the needs of the gay community.'

Meanwhile work resumed on *The Mirror Has Two Faces*. Written by Richard LaGravanese, who had scripted *The Fisher*

King, the plot by now scarcely resembled the French original which had starred Michèle Morgan as the plain-looking woman (it had been an effort for the make-up department to make Morgan look less than gorgeous) trapped in a loveless marriage. After being disfigured in a car crash she undergoes plastic surgery, emerges beautiful, and elopes with her more caring brother-in-law whilst the philandering husband exacts his revenge by shooting the surgeon.

Barbra wanted her version of the story to be a sequel to *The Way We Were*, that of the *mieskeit* who seduces the handsome hero, but only by the attractiveness of her inner self, her personality. In the reworked script, however, LaGravanese not only 'borrows' the celebrated French star's surname – Barbra's character becomes college professor, Rose Morgan – he allows Rose's self-confidence to plummet as she tries to come to terms with her newly-acquired beauty. The film was given a sterling cast. Jeff Bridges played Gregory Larkin, the fellow professor who enters a platonic marriage with Rose, only to find himself wanting her sexually after she has gone under the knife. Lauren Bacall played her mother and Pierce Brosnan, the dashing Irish-born actor who had recently triumphed as James Bond in *GoldenEye*, was second male lead. Other parts went to Mimi Rogers and Brenda Vaccaro. British star Dudley Moore was to have played Henry, Gregory's loquacious drinking pal, but he and Barbra apparently did not get on, and one week into shooting he was replaced by her *Owl And The Pussycat* co-star, George Segal. There were also on-set blues with the editor, who was fired, and the Director of Photography, Dante Spinotti, who left taking his entire crew with him. Barbra replaced him with Andrzej Barkowiak, who had filmed *Nuts*.

Between them, Barbra and Richard LaGravanese had turned a fine drama into a brash, semi-screwball comedy which lacks the simplistic charm and atmospheric ambience of the original and just does not work, though it is by no means 'the piece of shit' denounced by a crestfallen Larry Kramer. Even so, it was

savaged by the critics, lost money at the box office (subsequently recovered by video sales and rentals), and probably
would have sent Barbra's own self-confidence plunging to the
depths had it not been for the fact that at the time of its release,
in November 1996, there was someone very special in her life
to whom she could turn for comfort.

James Brolin, a 6 foot 4 inch Los Angeles-born actor, very
reminiscent of cowboy star Clint Walker, to whom he had often
been compared at the start of his career in the early 1960s, had
only hit the big time in Hollywood after gaining acclaim as the
junior partner in the *Marcus Welby MD* television series, which
ran from 1969 to 1976. Brolin's portrayal of Clark Gable in the
1975 film *Gable And Lombard* (opposite Jill Clayburgh) had,
however, brought more than its share of ridicule. Even the
renowned critic, Pauline Kael, who admitted that Brolin had
physically and vocally offered a fair imitation of Gable, had
been unable to resist adding, 'He's primarily a TV actor – you
can watch him with only half an eye and ear and not miss a
thing...He lacks what was the essence of Gable's appeal, his
cocksure masculinity.'

Two years Barbra's senior, very distinguished-looking with
prematurely white hair, James Brolin had first met Barbra on 1
July 1996 courtesy of a blind date organised by her friend
Christine, Jon Peters' ex-wife. Her first words to him, she
claimed during an interview on television's *The Rosie
O'Donnell Show*, were perhaps typical of her natural but zany
humour – 'Who screwed up your hair?'

The pair – regarded by many as an unlikely match considering some of Barbra's younger, less-virile-looking conquests – hit
it off at once and again the gossip columnists went into over-
drive. When they appeared together on *The Barbra Walters
Show* in November 1997 and Barbra told her hostess and millions of viewers, 'For the first time in my life, I'm not afraid to
love', the hacks began hacking. Brolin had been married twice
before – to Jane Cameron Agee, the mother of his grown-up

sons Josh and Jess – and to the actress Jan Smithers, whom he had divorced in 1995, the same year his first wife had been killed in a car crash. *The Los Angeles Daily News*' Marilyn Beck and Stacy Jenel Smith, in their eagerly awaited annual *Tacky Taste Awards* did not believe in fairytale romances for the middle-aged couples and awarded Barbra a gong, 'For her stomach-churning performance, acting like a sex-starved teeny-bopper...fawning and pawing her current stud muffin James Brolin, both of them nauseating everyone.'

The relationship was no media-hyped flash in the pan. On Wednesday 1 July 1998, the second anniversary of their blind date, in an evening ceremony at her Malibu home, conducted by Rabbi Beerman, Barbra Streisand became Brolin's third wife. Brolin's actor son, Josh, was best man and the bride, wearing white, was given away by her son Jason. Her half-sister Rose was bridesmaid, and other family members included Barbra's elder brother, Sheldon, and her eighty-nine-year-old mother Diana, now mostly confined to a wheelchair and said to be in the early stages of Alzheimer's disease. The 105 celebrity guests included the Bergmans, Jon Peters, Tom Hanks and his wife, Steven Spielberg and the Travoltas. Marvin Hamlisch conducted the sixteen-piece orchestra, and Barbra sang two brand new love songs to her groom: Melissa Manchester's 'Just One Lifetime' and Rolf Lovland's 'I've Dreamed Of You'.

Neither was the occasion minus the usual Streisand wackiness, though Barbra's decision to prevent press helicopters from intruding on the ceremony – by having her staff arrange massive stadium speakers in the grounds of her house, pointing them skywards and blasting out 2,000 watts of heavy metal music – was more out of necessity that her acting the clown. This was an intensely private moment to be shared only by those she cared about. Just one photographer was allowed – Barbra's friend, Deborah Wald. According to some reports, *People* magazine had paid Barbra $1 million for exclusive picture rights.

In keeping with modern Hollywood tradition, Barbra is thought to have persuaded James Brolin to sign a pre-nuptial agreement (or so declared the not-so-reliable *Star*), wherein should they separate he would receive $1 million as a payoff, and $300,000 a year for each year they remained married before divorcing. The wittiest agreement, probably just as 'authentic' as the one in the *Star*, had appeared four months earlier in *Vanity Fair*, and part-referred to Barbra's legendary long talons: 'the First Party shall be in no way liable for potential injury to the body of the Second Party resulting from contact with the fingernails of the First Party.' The secret honeymoon, according to the even less reliable *National Enquirer*, constituted a trip along the California coast in a $5,000 a day hired yacht.

Barbra's most recent album, *Higher Ground*, which had entered the *Billboard* chart at Number One towards the end of 1997, had been inspired by her friendship with President Clinton's elderly mother, Virginia Kelley, and Kelley's subsequent death and the Southern spirituals sung at the January 1994 funeral. Although the two had only known each other a year, such had been their rapport that Barbra had baptised her 'my Southern mum'. Kelley had also ended their every conversation on the telephone with the words 'I love you', something Barbra's own mother had apparently rarely or never done. *Higher Ground* had been dedicated to Virginia Kelley and had opened with 'I Believe/You'll Never Walk Alone', inspirational anthems, the latter from *Carousel*, which had helped American show business legend Jane Froman pick up the threads of her career immediately after World War II when she had been crippled in an air crash. There was also 'Deep River', the definitive version of which had been sung by another great fighter against oppression, Paul Robeson, while the album closed with a Hebrew *chesed*, Max Janowski's 'Avinu Malkeinu', offering a rare religious statement of which Barbra had said, '"Our Father, Our King" is a supplication to God to treat us with kindness and generosity, even when we haven't always lived up to His ideals for us.'

Barbra's new album – her last to date – was recorded in numerous studios between November 1998 and March 1999 – an unusually long time for her. *A Love Like Ours* was inspired, of course, by her new-found joy. 'Happiness *makes* you want to sing,' she said at the time. 'You know all those corny things they say in every love song you've ever heard? Well, they're true!'

TWO

THE MUSIC

This discography includes CD rereleases of original vinyl albums. 'BB' relates to the highest position reached in the US Billboard chart.

I Can Get It For You Wholesale
(Original Broadway Cast Recording)

Columbia 53020 (Original release 4/62) BB125

Overture/I'm Not A Well Man*/The Way Things Are/When Gemini Meets Capricorn/Momma, Momma, Momma/The Sound Of Money/Too Soon/The Family Way/Who Knows?/Ballad Of The Garment Trade*/Have I Told You Lately?/A Gift Today/Miss Marmelstein*/A Funny Thing Happened/What's In It For Me?/Eat A Little Something/What Are They Doing To Us?*

Music & lyrics: Harold Rome

* Streisand sings only on these tracks.

Most of these songs are instantly forgettable, with the exception of Streisand's showstopper, 'Miss Marmelstein', itself only remarkable on account of the wit and unprecedented vigour of her performance.

Pins And Needles (25th Anniversary Edition Of The Hit Musical Revue)

Columbia 57380 (Original release 5/62) Did not chart

Sing Me A Song With Social Significance/Doing The Reactionary*/One Big Union For Two/It's Better With A Union Man/Nobody Makes A Pass At Me*/I've Got The Nerve To Be In Love/Not Cricket To Picket*/Back To Work/Status Quo*/When I Grow Up (The G-Man Song)/Chain Store Daisy/Four Little Angels Of Peace*/Sunday In The Park/What Good Is Love*/Mene, Mene, Tekel

Music & lyrics: Harold Rome
* Streisand sings only on these tracks.

Again a forgettable collection of largely raucous neo-vaudeville tunes, none of which have survived the passage of time. Streisand appeared on this and the previous album, despite not being contracted to Columbia until October 1962.

The Barbra Streisand Album

Columbia 57374 (Original release 2/63) BB8

Cry Me A River/My Honey's Loving Arms/I'll Tell The Man In The Street/A Taste Of Honey/Who's Afraid Of The Big Bad Wolf?/Soon It's Gonna Rain/Happy Days Are Here Again/Keepin' Out Of Mischief Now/Much More/Come To The Supermarket (In Old Peking)/A Sleepin' Bee

Streisand had wanted her debut album to comprise a recital at the Bon Soir, and tape recordings were made of her 5, 6, 7 November performances, subsequently

dismissed on account of poor acoustics and audience rowdiness. Bon Soir songs which did not make the album were 'Lover Come Back To Me', 'Value' from Harry Stoones, *Leonard Bernstein's 'My Name Is Barbra', and 'I Hate Music', Harold Arlen's 'Napoleon' and 'Right As Rain'. The superb 'A Sleepin' Bee' came from his Broadway musical* House Of Flowers. *The cover picture is from a Bon Soir performance.*

The Second Barbra Streisand Album

Columbia 57378 (Original release 8/63) BB2

Any Place I Hang My Hat Is Home/Tight As The Rain/Down With Love/Who Will Buy?/When The Sun Comes Out/Gotta Move/My Colouring Book/ I Don't Care Much/Lover Come Back To Me/ I Stayed Too Long At The Fair/Like A Straw In The Wind

The album again featured songs Streisand had been performing in her Greenwich Village recitals, including 'Right As Rain' and 'Lover Come Back To Me', which she had wanted on her debut album. The Streisand interpretation of 'I Stayed Too Long At The Fair' is positively awesome. 'My Colouring Book' was her first general release single. Peter Matz's 'Gotta Move' was one of the first songs written especially for her.

Barbra Streisand: The Third Album

Columbia 57379 (Original release 2/64) BB5

My Melancholy Baby/Just In Time/Taking A Chance On Love/Bewitched, Bothered And Bewildered/

Never Will I Marry/As Time Goes By/Draw Me A
Circle/It Had To Be You/Make Believe/I Had Myself
A True Love

*Many critics regarded this to be Streisand's classiest
album so far. The songs, mostly earlier Broadway show-
stoppers, only make one wonder how stupendous she
would have sounded in the original productions at a
time when leading ladies were not always renowned for
vocal technique. 'My Melancholy Baby' takes the breath
away, and the* Casablanca *theme 'As Time Goes By' has
rarely sounded better. The later edition cover photograph, taken by Roddy McDowell for his famous* Double
Exposure *volume, was snapped during Streisand's
October 1963 guest slot on* The Judy Garland Show.

Funny Girl (Original Broadway Cast Recording)

Angel 64661 (Original release 4/64) BB2

Overture/If A Girl Isn't Pretty/I'm The Greatest
Star*/Cornet Man*/Who Taught Her
Everything?/His Love Makes Me Beautiful*/
I Want To Be Seen With You Tonight*/Henry
Street/People*/You Are Woman*/Don't Rain On
My Parade*/Sadie, Sadie*/Find Yourself A Man/Rat-
Tat-Tat-Tat*/Who Are You Now*/The Music That
Makes Me Dance*/Don't Rain On My Parade
(Reprise)*

Music: Jule Styne
Lyrics: Bob Merrill
  * Streisand sings only on these tracks.

*This album was recorded in a single session on 5 April
1964 which is reported to have been fraught with*

difficulty, which shows. The attendant Life *magazine reporter observed of Streisand, 'She was an hour late, but entered the room full of irritable musicians with the confidence of [circus trainer] Clyde Beatty. You could almost see the cane chair and whip…but when she sang she was a complete pro.'*

People

Columbia 9015 (Original release 9/64) BB1

Absent Minded Me/When In Rome (I Do As The Romans Do)/Fine And Dandy/Supper Time/Will He Like Me?/How Does The Wine Taste?/I'm All Smiles/Autumn/My Lord And Master/Love Is A Bore/Don't Like Goodbyes/People

Streisand's first album to top the Billboard *chart, ousting the Beatles'* A Hard Day's Night. *Most of the songs are little-heard standards which she revived, though only 'People', with its new arrangement and muted ending, may be regarded as definitive, perhaps with 'My Lord And Master' from* The King and I, *which here becomes almost a pop song.*

My Name Is Barbra

Columbia 9136 (Original Release 5/65) BB2

My Name Is Barbra/A Kid Again – I'm Five/Jenny Rebecca/My Pa/Sweet Zoo/Where Is The Wonder?/I Can See It/Someone To Watch Over Me/I've Got No Strings/If You Were The Only Boy In The World/Why Did I Choose You?/My Man

This was the first of two album tie-ins for Streisand's 60-minute CBS television special of the same name. 'My Man' (Mon Homme) created by Mistinguett in 1920 and reprised by Fanny Brice, was only sung in the final New York performance of Funny Girl. *In it Streisand completely eschews the simplistic style of the original, pulling out all the stops in such a way that it almost becomes* her *property. Aside from this, the finest interpretation here is undoubtedly 'Why Did I Choose You?', Streisand's very own* hymne à l'amour.

My Name Is Barbra, Two

Columbia 9209 (Original release 11/65) BB2

He Touched Me/The Shadow Of Your Smile/Quiet Night/I Got Plenty Of Nothin'/How Much Of The Dream Comes True/Second Hand Rose/The Kind Of Man A Woman Needs/All That I Want/Where's That Rainbow?/No More Songs For Me/MEDLEY: Second Hand Rose/Give Me The Simple Life/I Got Plenty Of Nothin'/Brother Can You Spare A Dime?/Nobody Knows You When You're Down And Out/Second Hand Rose/The Best Things In Life Are Free

The second of the tie-in albums for Streisand's first television special gets off to a fine start, though aside from the numbers contained in the medley the only well-known songs at the time were Fanny Brice's 'Second Hand Rose', 'I Got Plenty Of Nothin', and Sandpiper *theme 'The Shadow Of Your Smile'. 'He Touched Me', from Elliott Gould's flop musical* Drat! The Cat!, *almost certainly would have been assigned to obscurity had she not recorded it.*

Color Me Barbra

Columbia 9728 (Original release 3/66) BB3

Yesterdays/One Kiss/The Minute Waltz/Gotta
Move/Non C'est Rien*/Where Or When/CIRCUS
MEDLEY: Animal Crackers In My Soup—Funny Face
—That Face—They Didn't Believe Me—Were Thine
That Special Face—I've Grown Accustomed To Her
Face—Let's Face The Music And Dance—Sam, You
Made The Pants Too Long—What's New
Pussycat?—Small World—I Love You—I Stayed Too
Long At The Fair—Look At That Face/C'est Si Bon*/
Where Am I Going?/Starting Here, Starting Now
* Sung in French

*The album tie-in for Streisand's second television special.
Joss Basselli's 'Non C'est Rien' is the superb French original of 'Free Again'. 'The Minute Waltz' (Streisand stretch-
es this to almost two) is a hilarious parody on the classical piece by Chopin.*

Harold Sings Arlen (With Friend)

Columbia 52722 (Original release 3/66) Did not chart

Blues In The Night/Little Biscuit/Ding-Dong! The
Witch Is Dead*/A Sleepin' Bee/In The Shade Of the
New Apple Tree/Hit The Road To Dreamland/
Ac-Cent Tchu-Ate The Positive/My Shining
Hour/Today I Love Everybody/House Of
Flowers*/For Every Man There's A Woman/That's A
Kind Of Freedom

Music & Lyrics: Harold Arlen
* Streisand sings only on these tracks, the others are
duets with the composer

Streisand called Arlen 'The greatest composer of American music next to George Gershwin'. He remarked, 'Barbra's version of "House of Flowers" is the most moving, exciting rendition imaginable…I'm gratulant and grateful and an indebted idolater.'

Je M'Appelle Barbra

Columbia 9347 (Original release 11/66) BB5

Free Again/Autumn Leaves/What Now My Love/Ma Premiere Chanson/Clopin–Clopant/Le Mur/I Wish You Love/Speak To Me Of Love/Love And Learn/Once Upon A Summertime/Martina/I've Been Here

Streisand recorded additional songs, 'Les Enfants Qui Pleurant' (Martina), 'Et La Mer', along with 'Non C'est Rien' (Free Again) for her En Francais EP released in France, July 1966. Michel Legrand, the conductor and arranger, had recently enjoyed huge international acclaim with his score for the film Les Parapluies de Cherbourg, though Streisand was not permitted to include any of this on the album. 'Autumn Leaves' and 'Le Mur' were Piaf songs – the English language version of the latter, also here, had been covered by Sammy Davis Jr. 'What Now, My Love?', by Gilbert Becaud, began life as 'Et Maintenant'. 'Clopin-Clopant' had been introduced by future co-star Yves Montand. 'Speak To Me Of Love' is Jean Lenoir's enchanting 'Parlez-moi d'Amour' created by Lucienne Boyer in 1930. 'Ma Premiere Chanson' is self-composed with French lyrics by Eddy Marnay. Streisand's French is far from perfect, yet it is hard to believe she is actually singing phonetically.

Simply Streisand

Columbia 9482 (Original release 11/67) BB12

My Funny Valentine/The Nearness Of You/When
Sunny Gets Blue/Make The Man Love Me/Lover
Man (Oh, Where Can You Be?)/More Than You
Know/I'll Know/All The Things You Are/The Boy
Next Door/Stout-Hearted Men

*Streisand's first attempt at straight, unembellished stan-
dards with jazz-like introductions and schmaltzy
arrangements, far removed from her regular power-
house style, proved her least successful so far, although
it peaked at Number 12 in the Billboard chart. 'Stout-
Hearted Men', from Sigmund Romberg's operetta The
New Moon, was released as a single and, with
Streisand unashamedly imitating Mae West, became
the anthem in gay clubs across America (she also par-
odied West in her television special, The Belle of 14th
Street, filmed in March 1967, singing 'A Good Man Is
Hard To Find'). 'When Sunny Gets Blue' was a remnant
from her early nightclub repertoire.*

Barbra Streisand: A Christmas Album

Columbia 9557 (Original release 11/67) BB1 (Seasonal)

Jingle Bells/Have Yourself A Merry Little Christmas/
The Christmas Song/White Christmas/ My
Favourite Things/The Best Gift/Sleep In Heavenly
Peace/Ava Maria (Gounod)/O Little Town Of
Bethlehem/I Wonder As I Wander/The Lord's Prayer

*The controversy here centred around Streisand's
immensely self-publicised Jewishness and the fact that*

Right and below The early
faces of Streisand, in the late 60s
and early 70s.

Above Backstage, c. 1972.

Above With Robert Redford on the set of *The Way We Were*.

Below Movie still from *Funny Girl*, the point at which Streisand's star began to shine.

Left A rare shot of Streisand with the diva's diva, Judy Garland.

Below With Gene Hackman on the set of *All Night Long*.

Right An uncharacteristically flamboyant Streisand hams it up.

Left Streisand – known for valuing her privacy – in full 'Greta Garbo' mode.

Left and below
Streisand's relationships
have never charted a
steady course. Seen here
with ex-husband Elliot
Gould (left) and more
recent lover Don
Johnson (below).

Above left, above right and below Streisand's film career has been nothing if not eclectic. Seen here with Mandy Patinkin in her labour of love *Yentl* (above left), with Kris Kristofferson in the remake of *A Star Is Born* (above right), and with Ryan O'Neal in Peter Bogdanovich's *What's Up Doc?* (below).

The turn of the century saw a more confident, relaxed Streisand, pictured here with James Brolin at the Golden Globe awards.

she had recorded religious as well as secular seasonal favourites – additionally, that the session had had to take place in London because US Columbia executives, themselves mostly Jewish, would not permit this in the US. There were also objections to the cover, taken during the Central Park concert rehearsal, which depicted Streisand 'in holy pose' in the centre of a starburst. Some radio stations refused to play the album, which topped the Billboard *chart – the fans obviously did not care what religion Streisand was. Her hugely camped-up 'Jingle Bells' was again much favoured in gay clubs and bars.*

Funny Girl (Original Film Soundtrack)

Columbia 3220 (Original release 8/68) BB12

Overture/I'm The Greatest Star*/If A Girl Isn't Pretty/Roller Skate Rag*/I'd Rather Be Blue Over You*/His Love Makes Me Beautiful*/People*/You Are Woman, I Am Man*/Don't Rain On My Parade*/Sadie, Sadie*/The Swan*/Funny Girl*/My Man*/Finale

* Streisand vocals on these tracks

Music: Jule Styne
Lyrics: Rob Merrill

The album was recorded on 5 April, ten days after the New York premiere, and rush-released into the shops. Even so it was pre-empted by the unbelievably bad Diana Ross & The Supremes Sing & Perform Funny Girl, *with sleeve notes by Styne and arrangements by Streisand's own Peter Matz. She is claimed to have said of Ross, 'Who the hell does she think she is? The world doesn't need another Streisand!'*

A Happening In Central Park

Columbia 9710 (Original release 9/68) BB30

I Can See It/Love Is Like A New Born Child/Folk
Monologue/Cry Me A River/People/He Touched
Me/MEDLEY: Marty The Martian — The Sound Of
Music — Mississippi Mud — Santa Claus Is Coming
To Town/Natural Sounds/Second Hand Rose/Sleep
In Heavenly Peace/Happy Days Are Here Again

*A well balanced, well sung (despite Streisand's nervous-
ness on account of a PLO death threat mere hours
before her performance) edited recital of the free concert of 17 June 1967. Who but Streisand would have
been able to get away with singing Christmas songs in
the middle of summer?*

What About Today?

Columbia 47014 (Original release 7/69) BB31

What About Today?/Ask Yourself Why/Honey
Pie/Punky's Dilemma/Until It's Time For You To
Go/That's A Fine Kind O' Freedom/Little Tin
Soldier/With A Little Help From My
Friends/Alfie/The Morning After/Goodnight

*This was Streisand's first foray into the pop-rock genre
and does not suit her – her fans were dismayed with the
change and the album subsequently only reached
Number 31 on the Billboard chart. Yet Streisand's version of Lennon and McCartney's 'Honey Pie', one of
three Beatles songs here, though extremely giddy,
is close to a definitive interpretation; her superb rendition of Buffy Sainte-Marie's 'Until It's Time For You To Go',*

compares only with Elvis Presley's; and Jimmy Webb's elegaic 'Little Tin Soldier' fitted in with Streisand's anti-Vietnam War stance.

Hello Dolly! (Original Film Soundtrack)

Philips 810368 (Original release 11/69) BB49

Just Leave Everything To Me*/It Takes a Woman/It Takes A Woman (reprise)*/Put On Your Sunday Clothes*/Ribbons Down My Back/Dancing*/Before The Parade Passes By*/Elegance/Love Is Only Love*/Hello Dolly!*/It Only Takes A Moment/So Long Dearie*/Finale*

* Streisand's vocals on these tracks

Music & Lyrics: Jerry Herman

Streisand duets with Louis Armstrong on the title track. The other artistes appearing on the recording are Michael Crawford, Marianne McAndrew, Walter Matthau, Danny Lockin.

Barbra Streisand's Greatest Hits

Columbia 9968 (Original release 1/70) BB32

People/Second Hand Rose/Why Did I Choose You?/He Touched Me/Free Again/Don't Rain On My Parade/My Colouring Book/Sam, You Made The Pants Too Long/My Man/Gotta Move/Happy Days Are Here Again

On A Clear Day You Can See Forever
(Original Film Soundtrack)

Columbia 57377 (Original Release 7/70) BB108

Hurry! It's Lovely Up Here!*/On A Clear Day**/
Love With All The Trimmings*/Melinda*/Go To
Sleep*/He Isn't You*/What Did I Have That I Don't
Have*/Come Back To Me**/On A Clear Day
(reprise)***

    * Sung by Streisand
   ** Sung by Yves Montand
 *** Sung by both
  Music: Burton Lane
 Lyrics: Alan Jay Lerner

> *Montand has the best songs in this, the first Streisand studio album not to make the Billboard top 100, notably the title track and 'Come Back To Me'. Even so, it should not be ignored. Two other songs omitted to tie in with director's cuts were 'Wait Till We're Sixty-Five' (duet with Larry Blyden and 'Who Is There Among Us Who Knows?' (duet with Jack Nicholson.)*

The Owl And The Pussycat
(Original Film Soundtrack)

Columbia Masterworks 30401 (LP) (Original release 1/71) BB186

The Confrontation/The Warmup/The
Seduction/The Morning After/The Reunion
Music & Lyrics: performed by Blood, Sweat & Tears

> *Something of a curio, thus far not released on CD. Streisand, as character Doris, performs dialogue only with George Segal as the character of Felix.*

Stoney End

Columbia 30378 (Original release 2/71) BB10

I Don't Know Where I Stand/Hands Off The Man
(Flim Flam Man)/If You Could Read My Mind/Just A
Little Lovin' (Early In The Mornin')/Let Me
Go/Stoney End/No Easy Way Down/Time And
Love/Maybe/Free The People/I'll Be Home

*The title track, written by the late, undeniably great
Laura Nyro, became Streisand's biggest-selling single
since 'People' in 1965. Streisand was unsure about the
concept of covering material by Nyro, Joni Mitchell,
Randy Newman, etc. She had already begun work on*
The Singer, *an album of most of the numbers only on
the proviso that the masters would be destroyed should
she change her mind about releasing the album. It subsequently reached Number 10 on the* Billboard *chart,
though many diehard fans disliked it.*

Barbra Joan Streisand

Columbia 30792 (Original release 8/71) BB11

Beautiful Love/Where You Lead/I Never Meant To
Hurt You/One Less Bell To Answer–A House Is
Not A Home/Space Captain/Since I Fell For You/
Mother/The Summer Knows/I Mean To
Shine/You've Got A Friend

*Streisand's 'return to form', or almost, with an eclectic
mixture of contemporary songs, some of which have
since become standards: Michel Legrand's 'The Summer
Knows', Burt Bacharach's 'A House Is Not A Home'.
Others, such as John Lennon's 'Mother', are probably
best forgotten.*

Live Concert At The Forum

Columbia 31760 (Original release 10/72) BB19

Sing-Make Your Own Kind Of Music/Starting Here, Starting Now/Don't Rain On My Parade/Monologue/On A Clear Day/Sweet Inspiration-Where You Lead/Didn't We/My Man/Stoney End/Sing–Happy Days Are Here Again/People

Streisand's second live concert album represents her end-of-show contribution to the 4-For-McGovern benefit concert at the 18,000-seater Los Angeles Forum, 15 April 1972. Always a staunch Democrat, she supported George McGovern's stand against the Vietnam War. Also on the bill were Carole King, James Taylor and Quincy Jones. The opening song, 'Sing' from Sesame Street, *was six-year-old son Jason's favourite at the time. The concert resulted in opposing (and winning) presidential candidate Richard Nixon placing Streisand's name on his 'political enemies' list.*

Barbra Streisand...And Other Musical Instruments

Columbia 32655 (Original release 11/73) BB64

Piano Practicing/I Got Rhythm/Johnny One Note–One Note Samba/Glad To Be Unhappy/People/Second Hand Rose/Don't Rain On My Parade/Don't Ever Leave Me/Monologue/By Myself/Come Back To Me/I Never Has Seen Snow/Lied: Auf Dem Wasser Zu Singen/The World Is A Concerto/Make Your Own Kind Of Music/The Sweetest Sounds

The album tie-in for the television special of 2 November 1973, the last in Streisand's CBS contract. Filmed in London, Ray Charles was special guest but does not appear on the album. 'One Note Samba' is accompanied by East Indian instruments, but 'The World Is A Concerto' saw Streisand singing to a cacophony of household appliances: whistling kettle, vacuum cleaner, washing machine, pop-up toaster, blender etc. Her final note on 'I Got Rhythm', at twenty-three seconds, beat the record for the longest sustained note, held by Yma Sumac.

The Way We Were (Film Soundtrack Recording)

Columbia 57381 (Original release 1/74) BB20

The Way We Were*/Red Sails In The Sunset/Look What I've Got/Like Pretty/River Stay Way From My Door/The Way We Were (Inst)/Katie/In The Mood/Did You Know It Was Me?/Remembering/Wrap Your Troubles In Dreams/The Way We Were*

* Streisand sings only on these tracks.

This album was released one week before the same title solo album.

The Way We Were

Columbia 32801 (Original release 1/74) BB1

Being At War With Each Other/Something So Right/The Best Thing You've Ever Done*/The Way We Were**/All In Love Is Fair/What Are You Doing The Rest Of Your Life?/Summer Me, Winter Me*/Pieces of Dreams*/I've Never Been A Woman Before*/MEDLEY: My Buddy–How About Me?

** recorded 12/9/73

The album title was temporarily retitled Barbra Streisand Featuring 'The Way We Were' & 'All Love Is Fair' *when the producer of the film filed a suit against Columbia Records for breach of contract, claiming the public would be coerced into buying the studio album under false pretences. Following an out-of-court settlement it was changed back again. It topped the* Billboard *chart whereas the soundtrack peaked at Number 20. Michel Legrand's 'What Are You Doing The Rest Of Your Life' had been issued as a single in 1969. Songs marked * are from the aborted album* The Singer. *The medley is from the television special,* The Belle Of 14th Street.

Butterfly

Columbia 33005 (Original release 10/74) BB13

Love In The Afternoon/Guava Jelly/Grandma's Hands/I Won't Last A Day Without You/Jubilation/ Simple Man/Life On Mars/Since I Don't Have You/ Crying Time/Let The Good Times Roll

Some of the better songs from the Peters–Streisand sessions did not make it on to the album: Carole King's 'You Light Up My Life', The Drifters' 1960s hit 'On Broadway' and, unforgivably, Billie Holiday's 'God Bless The Child'. As such, one is left with a puzzling mish-mash. 'Love In The Afternoon' gets things off to a sensual start, and 'Guava Jelly' pulls no punches with its allusion to semen. The Carpenters' 'I Won't Last A Day Without You' is lacklustre and David Bowie himself denounced her version of his 'Life On Mars' as 'bloody awful'. 'Jubilation', on the other hand, is awesome and evokes wonderful memories of Mahalia Jackson's strident gospel singing. Needless to say, there would be no more Peters albums.

Funny Lady (Film Soundtrack Recording)

Arista 19006 (Original release 3/75) BB6

Blind Date/More Than You Know/It's Only A Paper
Moon–I Like Him/It's Only A Paper Moon–I Like
Her*/I Found A Million Dollar Baby (In A Five & Ten
Cent Store)/So Long Honey Lamb/I Got A Code In
My Doze/Clap Hands, Here Comes Charley*/(It's
Gonna Be A) Great Day/How Lucky Can You
Get?/Am I Blue?/Isn't This Better?/If I Love Again/
Let's Hear It For Me/Me And My Shadow*/How
Lucky Can You Get (single mix)

* Streisand's vocals on these tracks.

*The new songs for the film were by John Kander and
Fred Ebb. 'I Found A Million Dollar Baby' is from Brice's
repertoire, but 'I Got A Code In My Doze' was introduced
by British star Gracie Fields in 1929. Prince Charles visited the set whilst Streisand was recording 'So Long
Honey Lamb'. The pair shared a pot of tea and she later
joked, 'Who knows? If I'd been nicer to him I might have
been the first real Jewish princess!'*

Lazy Afternoon

Columbia 33815 (Original release 10/75) BB12

Lazy Afternoon/My Father's Song/By The Way/
Shake Me, Wake Me (When It's Over)/I Never
Had It So Good/Letters That Cross In The Mail/
You And I/Moanin' Low/A Child Is Born/Widescreen

*Streisand had been impressed with singer-songwriter
Rupert Holmes' debut album,* Widescreen, *and invited
him to work on this and the score of* A Star Is Born. *It*

*was recorded in April 1975 in just three six-hour ses-
sions. Four Holmes songs are included; he would not
allow more 'for fear of over-exposure'. Streisand composed the music for 'By The Way'. The title track had
been introduced at London's Café de Paris by Marlene
Dietrich in 1954. 'A Child Is Born' should have augmented the abortion scene in* Up The Sandbox *but was
dropped. The Four Tops' hit 'Shake Me, Wake Me' was
Streisand's first experiment in disco and was huge on
the gay club circuit.*

Classic Barbra

CBS Masterworks 33452 (Original release 2/76) BB46

Debussy: Beau Soir/Canteloube: Brezairola/Wolf:
Verschwiegene Liebe/Fauré: Pavane/Faure: Après Un
Reve/Orff: In Trutina/Handel: Lascia ch'io pianga/
Schumann: Mondnacht/Handel: Dank sei Dir,
Herr/Ogerman: I Loved You

*A truly wonderful, aesthetic album so far removed from
anything Streisand had ever done before that Columbia
Records added a clause to her contract before recording
took place in April–May 1973 that it would have to sell
2.5 million copies to fulfil her contractual requirement. It
did, eventually, though it took almost three years for her
to allow its release. In the days before the worlds of pop-
rock and opera were freely allowed to conjoin, classical
enthusiasts denounced Streisand's 'encroachment' onto
their territory, whilst regular fans thought her mad. Of
particular note are the Canteloube and Wolf pieces,
whilst 'I Loved You' is conductor-arranger Ogerman's own
setting of a poem by Pushkin.*

A Star Is Born

Columbia 57375 (Original release 11/76) BB1

Watch Closely Now*/Queen Bee/Everything/Lost Inside You**/Hellacious Acres*/Love Theme From *A Star Is Born* (Evergreen)/The Woman In The Moon/I Believe In Love/Crippled Crow*/FINALE: With One More Look At You/Watch Closely Now/REPRISE: Evergreen

Initially Rupert Holmes was brought in to work on the soundtrack, but walked out on the production after an altercation with Jon Peters, who replaced him with Paul Williams. Holmes' aborted 'The Nick Of Time' and 'Love Out Of Time' were consigned to a Warner Bros vault, along with his lyrics to 'Everything'. His 'Lullaby For Myself' subsequently appeared on Streisand's Superman *album. The title track and 'Lost Inside Of You' were co-written by Streisand.*

Streisand Superman

Columbia 34830 (Original release 6/77) BB3

Superman/Don't Believe What You Read/Baby Me Baby/I Found You Love/Answer Me/My Heart Belongs To Me/Cabin Fever/Love Comes From Unexpected Places/New York State Of Mind/Lullaby For Myself

'Don't Believe What You Read' and 'Answer Me' were co-written by Streisand, the former in response to defamatory press articles penned about her, the latter for A Star Is Born — *like Rupert Holmes' 'Lullaby For Myself' not used in the film. 'New York State Of Mind'*

was a cover of the Billy Joel classic – as often in the past, she excels the original. The sleeve photographs included the famous Streisand 'butt shot' which led to her posing in similar attire (skimpy shorts, vest but without *socks and shoes) for the October 1977 cover of* Playboy.

Songbird

Columbia 35375 (Original release 5/78) BB12

Tomorrow/A Man I Loved/I Don't Break Easily/Love Breakdown/You Don't Bring Me Flowers (solo version)/Honey Can I Put On Your Clothes?/One More Night/Stay Away/Deep In The Night/Songbird

The first album from Streisand's renewed contract with Columbia Records which guaranteed her an advance of $1.5 million per album with a twenty per cent royalty. Undoubtedly the star track is her definitive version of Neil Diamond's 'You Don't Bring Me Flowers'. In the autumn of 1978 Gary Guthrie, a Louisville disc-jockey, 'played around' with Streisand and Diamond's versions of the song, creating an illegal duet which brought so many calls that the radio station switchboard was jammed. Rather than sue, Columbia brought the two together and they recorded an authentic duet which topped the US charts six weeks after its release. Streisand also recorded Elton John's 'Love Song' and the Beatles' 'Here, There And Everywhere', not included on the album.

Eyes Of Laura Mars (Film Soundtrack Album)

BB125 Columbia 35487 (Original release 7/78) Not re-released on CD
> Jon Peters produced the film, starring Faye Dunaway. Other artistes on the album are Odyssey, KC & The Sunshine Band, Michael Zaeger Band, Michalksy & Oosterveen. Streisand sings 'Prisoner'.

Barbra Streisand's Greatest Hits Volume 2

Columbia 35679 (Original release 11/78) BB1
> Evergreen/Prisoner/My Heart Belongs To Me/Songbird/You Don't Bring Me Flowers (with Neil Diamond)/The Way We Were/Sweet Inspiration—Where You Lead/All In Love Is Fair/Superman/Stoney End

> *Zoomed to the top of the* Billboard *chart in the wake of the success of the Neil Diamond song, selling four million copies and earning Streisand a cool $6 million. It was rumoured at the time that Streisand wanted to record and include a studio version of 'Hativka' (the Israeli National Anthem) which she had performed in May on ABC Television's* The Stars Salute Israel At 30.

The Main Event (Film Soundtrack Album)

Columbia 57376 (Original release 6/79) BB20
> The Main Event—Fight*/The Body Shop/The Main Event-Fight (short version)*/Copeland Meets The Coasters—Get A Job/Big Girls Don't Cry/It's Your Foot Again/Angry Eyes/I'd Clean A Fish For You/The Main Event*

> * Streisand's vocals on these tracks

The disco-style Paul Jabara–Bruce Roberts title track, performed here three times, replaced the ballads composed by Streisand to accompany lyrics by Alan and Marilyn Bergman and David Shire – the reason for the switch being that twelve-year-old son Jason preferred the up-tempo number.

Wet

Columbia 36258 (Original release 10/78) BB7

Wet/Come Rain Or Shine/Splish Splash/On Rainy Afternoons/After The Rain/No More Tears (Enough Is Enough) (duet with Donna Summer)/Niagara/I Ain't Gonna Cry Tonight/Kiss Me In The Rain

The theme here is of course water. Streisand co-wrote the title track. She had hired Paul Jarbara and Bruce Roberts to score The Main Event, *and following the success of the soundtrack they came up with 'Enough Is Enough', an 'unnatural' track in that as opposed to being recorded à la Streisand in a single take like the other songs on the album, technicians spent 150 hours and $100,000 remixing it. Fortunately it topped the US and most of the European charts, proving there is no accounting for taste. 'Tracks Of My Tears' was recorded, but not used.*

Guilty

Columbia 36750 (Original release 9/80) BB1

Guilty (duet with Barry Gibb)/Woman In Love/Run Wild/Promises/The Love Inside/What Kind Of Fool (duet with Barry Gibb)/Life Story/Never Give Up/Make It Like A Memory

Streisand's fifth Billboard *chart-topper, her biggest seller (twenty million copies worldwide) to date, though melodiously not on a par with her regular work. She hired Barry Gibb to write and produce, impressed by the Bee Gees' soundtrack for the disco phenomenon* Saturday Night Fever. *Initially he was reluctant, having heard of Streisand's reputation. She was difficult, but with reason – the Bee Gees' management demanded seventy-five per cent of the performance royalties, applying the theory that the group were three and she but one. She argued, 'They all sound alike!' and the royalties were shared 50–50. The duets with Gibb both reached the US Top Ten. 'Woman In Love' topped the US chart for three weeks. The French version, Nicole Croisille's 'Une Femme Amoureuse', topped the French chart.*

Memories

Columbia 37678 (Original release 11/81) BB6

Memory/You Don't Bring Me Flowers (duet with Neil Diamond)/My Heart Belongs To Me/New York State Of Mind/No More Tears (Enough Is Enough) (duet with Donna Summer)/Comin' In And Out Of Your Life/Evergreen (Love Theme from *A Star Is Born*)/Lost Inside Of You/The Love Inside/The Way We Were

All tracks previously released save 'Comin' In And Out Of Your Life' and 'Memory' – the latter from Andrew Lloyd Webber's Cats. *Released in Europe as* Barbra Streisand: Love Songs *with supplementary tracks 'Wet', 'A Man I Loved', 'I Don't Break Easily' and 'Kiss Me In The Rain'. It became a UK best-seller, but only reached Number 10 on the* Billboard *chart.*

Yentl (Original Film Soundtrack)

Columbia 39152 (Original release 11/83) BB9

Where Is It Written?/Papa, Can You Hear Me?/This Is One Of Those Moments/No Wonder/The Way He Makes Me Feel/No Wonder (Part Two)/ Tomorrow Night/Will Someone Ever Look At Me That Way?/No Matter What Happens/No Wonder (reprise)/A Piece Of Sky/The Way He Makes Me Feel*/No Matter What Happens*

* All but last two tracks recorded in London, early 1982.

The Legend Of Barbra Streisand: The Woman & Her Music In Her Own Words *was a double LP produced by Westwood One for Columbia, at around this time, for the promotion of* Yentl *and for radio play only. It contained a 60-minute interview by Mary Turner, and the following:* People/The Minute Waltz/Where Am I Going?/Second Hand Rose/My Man/He Touched Me/ Free Again/Sam, You Made The Pants Too Long/The Way We Were/All In Love Is Fair/ Evergreen/My Heart Belongs To Me/You Don't Bring Me Flowers/ Songbird/ No More Tears/Woman In Love/Guilty/ Papa, Can You Hear Me?/The Way He Makes Me Feel/Where Is It Written?/A Piece Of Sky

Emotion

Columbia 39480 (Original release 10/84) BB19

Emotion/Make No Mistake, He's Mine (duet with Kim Carnes)/Time Machine/Best I Could/Left In The Dark/Heart Don't Change My Mind/When I Dream/You're A Step In The Right Direction/Clear Sailing/Here We Are At Last

Part-produced (along with nine others, including Streisand, in thirteen locations) by Richard Baskin, from early 1984 the new man in her life who provided lyrics for 'Here We Are At Last', a melody she had originally composed for The Main Event. *Part of it also turns up in* Nuts. *Streisand is backed on the title track by the Pointer Sisters. Songs to date not released from the sessions are 'How Do You Keep The Music Playing?' and 'When The Lovin' Goes Out Of The Lovin''. There was also a limited edition picture disc. The single of 'Left In The Dark' was accompanied by Streisand's first six-minute monochrome promotional video, premiered on MTV.*

The Broadway Album

Columbia 40092 (Original release 11/85) BB1

Putting It Together/If I Loved You/Something's Coming/Not While I'm Around/Being Alive/I Have Dreamed–We Kiss In A Shadow–Something Wonderful/Adelaide's Lament/Send In The Clowns/Pretty Women–The Ladies Who Lunch/Can't Help Lovin' That Man/I Loves You Porgy-Porgy I's Your Woman Now/Somewhere

In the author's opinion, the best Streisand album ever. 'Can't Help Lovin' That Man', originally sung in Showboat *by Helen Morgan, has harmonica accompaniment by Stevie Wonder. 'Something's Coming' and 'Somewhere' are from* West Side Story. *'Adelaide's Lament', the novelty piece from* Guys And Dolls, *was only included on the CD. The 'I Have Dreamed' medley is part of a much longer sequence from* The King And I. *Of the more contemporary material Streisand favoured Stephen Sondheim. 'Pretty Woman' from his* Sweeney Todd *and*

'The Ladies Who Lunch' from Company *are perfectly combined. 'Not While I'm Around' is also from the former, 'Being Alive' from the latter. Streisand's reading of 'Send In The Clowns' (from* A Little Night Music*) is breathtaking. 'Putting It Together' was from Sondheim's current Broadway smash,* Sunday In The Park With George. *From Helen Morgan's* Showboat *proclamation, 'Can't Help Lovin' That Man', to the portentiousness of Sondheim's 'Send In The Clowns', by way of a superbly paced* Porgy And Bess *medley and a version of 'Somewhere' which becomes a symphonie en miniature, every track is a classic.*

NOTE: Twenty-three songs were recorded in the sessions of July–August 1985, originally for issue as a double album. Columbia, who opposed the concept in any way or form, figured this would be too risky and a single forty-five-minute maximum album compromise was reached. Again, the company imposed the conditions they had with Classical Barbra *in that 2.5 million copies would have to be sold to earn Streisand's contractual requirements. It did – the advance orders alone totalled 850,000. Other songs recorded but not released include 'Home', 'Shall We Dance?–Hello Young Lovers', 'Show Me', 'An Unusual Way', 'Being Good Isn't Enough', 'A Quiet Thing–There Won't Be Trumpets'. The latter song had already been recorded and dropped, in 1974 when Streisand had thought of including it on* Butterfly.

One Voice

Columbia 40788 (Original release 4/87) BB9

Somewhere/Evergreen/Something's Coming/
People/Send In The Clowns/Over The Rainbow/
Guilty (with Barry Gibb)/Papa, Can You Hear

Me?/The Way We Were/It's A New World/Happy
Days Are Here Again/America The Beautiful

*Streisand's third live concert album, produced by Richard
Baskin and recorded at her Malibu home in support of
the Democratic senatorial campaign in the wake of the
Chernobyl disaster, which she blamed partly on
Reagan's Republican pro-armament policies. She said
that her favourite Judy Garland number, 'Over The
Rainbow', with its wonderfully human lyrics and rarely-
heard verse, seemed perfect as 'an expression of hope
for the future of the planet'. Her second Garland song
of the evening was 'It's A New World', from the 1954
version of* A Star Is Born. *The final song was taken from
the previous evening's dress rehearsal because, the
emotion proving too much for her, Streisand had forgotten the words. 'Papa, Can You Hear Me?', from Yentl, was
announced as a tribute 'to those great father figures
Abraham Lincoln, John F. Kennedy, Ghandi and Sadat'.*

Nuts (Film Soundtrack Album)

Columbia 40876 (Original release 12/87) Did not chart

Claudia's Theme & Variations/The Apartment/The
Bar/The Hospital/The Finale/End Credits

*Dissatisfied with the original score for the film, Streisand
composed a beautifully atmospheric new one, the first
time she had done this. It was issued on a limited edition
album, tape and CD. The final track was later given words
by Alan and Marilyn Bergman and became 'Two People'.*

Till I Loved You

Columbia 40880 (Original release 10/88) BB10

The Place You Find Love/On My Way To You/Till I
Loved You (with Don Johnson)/Love Light/All I Ask
Of You/You And Me For Always/Why Let It
Go?/Two People/What Were We Thinking Of?/
Some Things Never Last/One More Time Around

*Interesting in that the producers include Quincy Jones,
Burt Bacharach, Carole Bayer Sager and Streisand herself. Otherwise a pretty bland clutch of contemporary
songs. Even Michel Legrand's 'On My Way To You' is not
up to his usual high standard. The title track, Streisand's
positively awful duet with Don Johnson – he cannot
sing! – was from an unproduced pop opera,* Goya, A
Life, *by tenor Placido Domingo. The mind boggles. 'Two
People' was revived from the scores of* Nuts. *'All I Ask Of
You' is from* The Phantom Of The Opera. *The backing
vocals on 'The Place You Find Love' include Dionne
Warwick and Luther Vandross.*

A Collection: Greatest Hits...And More

Columbia 45369 (Original release 10/89) BB26

We're Not Makin' Love Anymore/Woman In
Love/All I Ask Of You/Comin' In And Out Of Your
Life/What Kind Of Fool (with Barry Gibb)/The Main
Event–Fight/Someone That I Used To Love/By The
Way/Guilty (with Barry Gibb)/Memory/The Way
He Makes Me Feel (studio version)/Somewhere

*Mostly previously released material. Only 'We're Not
Makin' Love' and 'Someone That I Used To Love' were
newly recorded.*

Just For The Record (4-CD Boxed Gift Set)

Columbia 44111 (Original release 9/91) BB38
A collection of out-takes and rarities.
DISC 1: The 1960s Part One
You'll Never Know*/A Sleepin' Bee/Moon
River/Miss Marmelstein/Happy Days Are Here
Again/Keepin' Out Of Mischief Now**/I Hate
Music**/Nobody's Heart (Belongs To
Me)**/Value**/Cry Me A River**/Who's Afraid Of
The Big Bad Wolf?**/I Had Myself A True
Love**/Lover, Come Back To Me**/Spring Can
Really Hang You Up The Most/My Honey's Loving
Arms/Any Place I Hang My Hat Is Home/When The
Sun Come Out/Be My Guest***/MEDLEY: Hooray
For Love–After You've Gone–By Myself–'S
Wonderful–(I Like New York In June) How About
You?–Lover, Come Back
* Streisand's first amateur recording, taped with
'Zing! Went The Strings Of My Heart' (unreleased
to date), 29 December 1955 when she was only
thirteen.
** Recorded at New York's Bon Soir Club, 1962.
*** Dialogue with Judy Garland & Ethel Merman
October 1963.
DISC 2: The 1960s Part Two
I'm The Greatest Star*/My Man–Auld Lang
Syne*/People/Second Hand Rose**/MEDLEY:
Second Hand Rose–Give Me The Simple Life–Any
Place I Hang My Hat Is Home–Nobody Knows You
(When You're Down And Out)–Second Hand
Rose–The Best Things In Life Are Free***/1965
Emmy Awards/He Touched Me/You Wanna
Bet/House Of Flowers/Ding-Dong! The Witch Is
Dead (with Harold Arlen)/I Stayed Too Long At The

Fair–Look At That Face/Starting Here, Starting
Now/A Good Man Is Hard To Find–Some Of These
Days/I'm Always Chasing Rainbows/ Sleep In
Heavenly Peace/Don't Rain On My Parade/ Funny
Girl/1969 Academy Awards/Friars Club Tributes
(Harold Arlen–Jule Styne–Don Rickles–Richard
Rodgers)/Hello, Dolly! (with Louis Armstrong)/On A
Clear Day (You Can See Forever)/When You Gotta
Go–In the Wee Small Hours Of The Morning.

* Extracts from the 26 December 1966 closing night
of the New York *Funny Girl.*

** Sung by Diana Kind, Streisand's mother.

*** Act II Medley from television special *My Name Is
Barbra.*

DISC 3: The 1970s

The Singer/I Can Do It/Stoney End/Close To You
(with Burt Bacharach)/We've Only Just Begun/Since
I Fell For You/You're The Top (with Ryan O'Neal)/
What Are You Doing The Rest Of Your Life? (with
Michel Legrand)/If I Close My Eyes/Between
Yesterday And Tomorrow/Can You Tell The
Moment?/The Way We Were (soundtrack version)/
Cryin' Time (with Ray Charles)/God Bless The
Child/ A Quiet Thing–There Won't Be
Trumpets/Lost Inside Of You (soundtrack alternative
version)/ Evergreen (demo soundtrack)/1977
Academy Awards/Hatikvah*

* Israeli National Anthem. Extract from *The Stars
Salute Israel At 30*, preceded by satellite link
conversation with Golda Meir.

DISC 4: The 1980s

You Don't Bring Me Flowers (with Neil
Diamond)/The Way We Weren't–The Way We
Were (live)/Guilty (with Barry Gibb)/Papa, Can You
Hear Me? (demo)/The Moon And I (demo)/A Piece

Of Sky (demo)/I Know Him So Well/If I Loved You/Putting It Together/Over The Rainbow/Theme From Nuts/Here We Are At Last/Warm All Over/You'll Never Know.

A truly spectacular retrospective, with around 50 previously unreleased items, which enables the listener to mature with Barbra's changing timbre and musical tastes from age thirteen to almost fifty. The set contains a ninety-two page booklet written by her, along with 150 photographs from her private collection, complete with frequently revealing and amusing little anecdotes. There are Streisand's first accompanist Howard Jeffrey, who died of AIDS in 1988; Gracie Davidson, her housekeeper; her mother, Diana Kind, who had recently undergone heart bypass surgery; Cis Corman, described as 'my best friend through the 60s, 70s and 80s'. In 1998 the package was re-released in a smaller double jewelbox, with two booklets totalling fifty-six pages, the text of which was abridged.

The Prince Of Tides (Film soundtrack album)

Columbia 48627 (Original release 11/91) BB84

Main Title/Teddy Bears/To New York/The Bloodstain/The Fishmarket/The New York Willies/The Village Walk/Lilia's Theme/Home Movies/Daddy's Home/The Hallway (Love Theme)/They Love You Dad/So Cruel/Savannah Awakes/Love Montage/Tom Comes Home/The Outdoors/Tom's Breakdown/The Street/For All We Know (instrumental)/The Reunion/End Credits/For All We Know*/Places That Belong To You*

* Streisand vocals on these tracks only.

John Barry should have been the composer, but after an on-set argument with Streisand he was replaced by James Newton Howard, who had worked with her on the Songbird *and* Emotion *albums.*

Highlights From Just The Record

Columbia 52849 (Original release 6/92) did not chart

You'll Never Know/A Sleepin' Bee/Miss Marmelstein/I Hate Music/Nobody's Heart (Belongs To Me)/Cry Me A River/Get Happy–Happy Days Are Here Again (with Judy Garland)/People/Second Hand Rose (Diana Kind)/MEDLEY from *My Name Is Barbra*/You Wanna Bet/Come Rain Or Come Shine (Harold Arlen)/Monologue (Don Rickles)/The Sweetest Sounds (Richard Rodgers)/You're The Top (with Ryan O'Neal)/What Are You Doing The Rest Of Your Life? (with Michel Legrand)/Cryin' Time (with Ray Charles)/A Quiet Thing–There Won't Be Trumpets/Evergreen (demo)/Between Yesterday And Tomorrow/You Don't Bring Me Flowers (with Neil Diamond)/Papa, Can You Hear Me? (demo)/I Know Him So Well/Warm All Over/You'll Never Know

Back To Broadway

Columbia 44189 (Original release 6/93) BB1

Some Enchanted Evening/Everybody Says Don't/The Music Of The Night (with Michael Crawford)/Speak Low/As If We Never Said Goodbye/Children Will Listen/I Have A Love–One Hand, One Heart (with Johnny Mathias)/I've Never

Been In Love Before/Luck Be A Lady/With One
Look/The Man I Love/Move On

*Streisand's 50th album, the first in a new contract with
Columbia's parent company, Sony, who signed her for a
staggering $60 million. The deal guaranteed an advance
of $5 million per album, plus forty-two per cent of the
wholesale price, around $2.50 for each unit sold. She
therefore decided to play safe, and this was the very
first Streisand album to enter the* Billboard *chart at
Number One. Though it did not sell as well as* The
Broadway Album, *it at least signalled her 'Children Will
Listen' (from* Into The Woods*); 'I Have A Love–One
Hand', a duet with Johnny Mathis from* West Side
Story*; 'Everybody Says Don't' (from* Anyone Can
Whistle*); 'Move On' (from* Sunday In The Park With
George*). 'As If We Never Said Goodbye' and 'With One
Look' were from Andrew Lloyd Webber's yet to be staged*
Sunset Boulevard. *'Luck Be A Lady', originally sung by
Marlon Brando, the Peggy Lee classic 'The Man I Love'
and Kurt Weill's gorgeous 'Speak Low' have rarely been
better performed.*

Duets (A Frank Sinatra Album)

Capitol 89611 (Original release 9/94)

*A 'fabricated' album of duets which surprised many
when Streisand agreed to record and forward her contribution to 'I've Got A Crush On You' so that Sinatra's
vocals could be added in a studio. Other performers in
tandem are Kenny G, Gloria Estefan, Bono, Tony Bennett
and Aretha Franklin.*

Barbra: The Concert (2-CD Set)

Columbia 66109 (Original release 9/94) BB10
        Disc One: ACT I
        Overture/As If We Never Said Goodbye/Opening
        Remarks/I'm Still Here-Everybody Says Don't–Don't
        Rain On My Parade/Can't Help Lovin' That Man/I'll
        Know (with Marlon Brando)/People/Lover Man/
        Therapist Dialogue No. 1/Will He Like Me?/
        Therapist Dialogue No. 2/He Touched Me/
        Evergreen/Therapist Dialogue No. 3/The Man That
        Got Away/On A Clear Day (You Can See Forever)
        Disc Two: ACT II
        Entr'acte/The Way We Were/You Don't Bring Me
        Flowers/Lazy Afternoon/DISNEY MEDLEY: Once
        Upon A Dream – When You Wish Upon A Star –
        Someday My Prince Will Come/Not While I'm
        Around/Ordinary Miracles/YENTL MEDLEY: Where
        Is It Written – Papa, Can You Hear Me? – Will
        Someone Ever Look At Me That Way? – A Piece Of
        Sky/Happy Days Are Here Again/My Man/For All
        We Know/Somewhere

Not the legendary New Year's Eve 1993 concert in Las Vegas (apart from the added Disney medley), but assembled extracts of June-July 1994 at New York's Madison Square Garden. The companion video was filmed at the Arrowhead Pond, Anaheim, outside Los Angeles on 22/24 July 1994. Quite simply, Streisand at her very best. Full details of the Las Vegas concert appear in the main text of this book.

The Concert: Highlights

Columbia 67100 (Original release 5/95) Did not chart
Overture/As If We Never Said Goodbye/Opening
Remarks/I'm Still Here–Everybody Says Don't–
Don't Rain On My Parade/Can't Help Lovin' That
Man/I'll Know/People/Will He Like Me?/He Touched
Me/Evergreen/The Man That Got Away/The Way
We Were/You Don't Bring Me Flowers/Lazy
Afternoon/Not While I'm Around/Ordinary
Miracles/YENTL MEDLEY/Happy Days Are Here
Again/My Man/Somewhere

The Mirror Has Two Faces (Film Soundtrack Album)

Columbia 67887 (Original release 11/96) BB7
Main Title/In Questa Reggia?/An Ad/In A
Sentimental Mood/Rose Sees Greg/Alex Hurts/The
Dating Montage/My Intentions?/You Picked Me!/A
Funny Kind Of Proposal/Picnic In The Park/Greg
Falls For Rose/Try A Little Tenderness (David
Sanborn)/The Mirror/Going Back To Mom/Rocking
In The Chair/The Power Inside Of Me (Richard
Marx)/Rose Leaves Greg/Ruby/Rose Dumps
Alex/Greg Claims Rose/The Apology–Nessun
Dorma (Luciano Pavarotti)/I Finally Found Someone
(Streisand duet with Bryan Adams)/All Of My Life
(Streisand)

*As usual, much of Streisand's magic is lost when she is
forced to 'downgrade' her voice to suit that of a less
potent performer – i.e., the duet with Adams. 'It Doesn't
Get Better Than This' was recorded for the soundtrack
but discarded.*

Higher Ground

Columbia 66181 (Original release 11/97) BB1

I Believe–You'll Never Walk Alone/Higher
Ground/At The Same Time/Tell Him (with Celine
Dion)/On Holy Ground/If I Could/Circle/The Water
Is Wide–Deep River/Leading Him With Your
Heart/Lessons To Be Learned/Everything Must
Change/Avinu Malkeinu

*A project inspired by the January 1994 funeral in
Arkansas of Virginia Kelley, President Clinton's mother, to
whom it is dedicated. It entered the* Billboard *chart at
Number One. 'I Believe–You'll Never Walk Alone', the latter from Rodgers & Hammerstein's* Carousel, *were
1950s hits for both Frankie Laine and Jane Froman. The
duet with Dion is marred by the latter's tendency to
shriek her top notes rather than sing them. 'Deep River'
is the Paul Robeson classic. 'Leading With Your Heart'
was also the title of Kelley's autobiography. 'On Holy
Ground' was the gospel song sung by Janice Sojstrand at
Kelley's funeral service. Streisand's rendition is intensely
moving.*

A Love Like Ours

Columbia 69601 (Original release 9/99) BB6

I've Dreamed Of You/Isn't It A Pity/The Island/Love
Like Ours/If You Ever Leave Me (with Vince
Gill)/We Must Be Loving Right/If I Never Met You/It
Must Be You/Just One Lifetime/If I Didn't Love
You/Wait/The Music That Makes Me Dance.

A concept not unlike, but far better than, the earlier

album with Don Johnson – save that this one focuses on the more positive aspects of a relationship which one hopes for Streisand will endure. Streisand sang 'I've Dreamed Of You' and 'Just One Lifetime' at her July 1998 wedding to actor James Brolin, who appears with her on the cover. George and Ira Gershwin's 'Isn't It A Pity' comes from their 1932 Broadway revue, Pardon My English. *'Wait' has music by old composer friend Michel Legrand. 'The Music That Makes Me Dance' is a revival of the song from* Funny Girl. *The songs are not overtly remarkable but the sentiments expressed are sincere and heartfelt. 'If You Ever Leave Me', her duet with Vince Gill, is a masterpiece, its lyrics reminiscent of Piaf's 'If You Love Me, Really Love Me'.*

SINGLES

This list comprises Streisand's 7-inch US vinyl singles released on Columbia (unless otherwise stated).

Miss Marmelstein(Streisand)/**Who Knows?**(Marilyn Cooper)
No serial number. Released 4/62.
Promo. From *I Can Get It For You Wholesale*. Did not chart.

Happy Days Are Here Again/When The Sun Comes Out
4–42631. Released 11/62.
Limited pressing of 500 copies only. Did not chart.

My Colouring Book/Lover, Come Back To Me
4-42648. Released 11/62
Did not chart.

People/I Am A Woman
4–42965. Released 1/64.
The B-side is the solo version of the Streisand–Sharif duet from *Funny Girl* which predates the cast album. BB5.

Absent Minded Me/Funny Girl
4–43128. Released 8/64.
Up-tempo version predating the film soundtrack. BB44.

Why Did I Choose You/My Love
4–43248. Released 3/65. Both songs from the musical *The Yearling*, the latter reappearing as 'My Pa' with new lyrics on *My Name Is Barbra*. BB77.

Happy Days Are Here Again/My Colouring Book
13–33078. Released 3/65. 'Hall of Fame' series, original 11/62 versions. Did not chart.

My Man/Where Is The Wonder?
4–43323. Released 6/65. BB79.

He Touched Me/I Like Him
4–43403. Released 9/65. Both songs from ill-fated musical *Drat! The Cat!* BB53.

Second Hand Rose/The Kind Of Man A Woman Needs
4–43469. Released 11/65. BB32.

Where Am I Going?/You Wanna Bet
4–43518. Released 1/66. BB94.

Sam, You Made The Pants Too Long/The Minute Waltz
4–43612. Released 4/66. BB98.

Non, C'est Rien/Le Mur
4–43739. Released 7/66. Did not chart.

Barbra Streisand En Francais
Tracks: Non, C'est Rien/Les Enfants Qui Pleurent*/Et La Mer*/Le Mur
CBS EP–6048. Released 7/66. French release with *unreleased songs from the *Je M'Appelle Barbra* sessions.

Free Again/I've Been Here (Le Mur)
4–43808. Released 9/66. BB83.

Sleep In Heavenly Peace/Ave Maria (Gounod)
4–43896. Released 11/66. Did not chart.

Stout-Hearted Men/Look
4–44225. Released 6/67. 'Look', previously unreleased, was from the *Je M'Appelle Barbra* sessions. BB92.

Lover Man/My Funny Valentine
4–44331. Released 10/67. Did not chart.

Jingle Bells/White Christmas
4–44350. Released 11/67. Radio promo only.

Have Yourself A Merry Little Christmas/The Best Gift
4–44351. Released 11/67. Radio promo only.

My Favourite Things/The Christmas Song
4–44352. Released 11/67. Radio promo only.

The Lord's Prayer/I Wonder As I Wander
4–44354. Released 11/67. Radio promo only.

Our Corner Of The Night/He Could Show Me
4–44474. Released 2/68. Not released on album. Did not chart.

The Morning After/Where Is The Wonder?
4–44532. Released 4/68. Did not chart.

Funny Girl/I'd Rather Be Blue Over You
4–44622. Released 7/68. Alternative versions of *Funny Girl* numbers, neither released on album, the former one minute longer than the original version. Did not chart.

My Man/Don't Rain On My Parade
4–44704. Released 11/68. The B-side, not released on album, contains a different ending. Did not chart.

Frank Mills/Punky's Dilemma
4–44775. Released 2/69. The A-side, unreleased on album, from the musical *Hair*. Did not chart.

Funny Girl/I'd Rather Be Blue Over You
13–33154. Released 5/69. 'Hall of Fame' series, original 7/68 versions. Did not chart.

My Man/Don't Rain On My Parade
13–33161. Released 6/69. 'Hall of Fame' series, original 11/68 versions. Did not chart.

Little Tin Soldier/Honey Pie
4–44921. Released 7/69. Did not chart.

What Are You Doing The Rest Of Your Life?/What About Today
4–45040. Released 10/69.

Before The Parade Passes By/Love Is Only Love
4–45072. Released 12/69. The first song is completely different from the version on the *Hello, Dolly!* soundtrack. Did not chart.

Hello, Dolly! (mono)/Hello, Dolly! (stereo)
Twentieth Century Fox Records 6714. Released 12/69. Promo. An edited version of the song including the duet segment with Louis Armstrong. It was later included in *Just For The Record*. Did not chart.

The Best Thing You've Ever Done/Summer Me, Winter Me
4–45147. Released 4/70. The former differs from the version on *The Way We Were* soundtrack. Did not chart.

On A Clear Day (mono)/On A Clear Day (stereo)
Columbia AE–24. Released 7/70. This version differs from that on the soundtrack. Did not chart.

Stoney End/I'll Be Home
4–45236. Released 9/70. BB6.

Time And Love/No Easy Way Down
4–45341. Released 2/71. The A-side has a different instrumental mix to that on *Stoney End*. BB51.

Flim Flam Man/Maybe
4–45384. Released 4/71. BB82.

Where You Lead/Since I Fell For You
4–45414. Released 6/71. BB40.

Stoney End/Time And Love
13–33199. Released 8/71. 'Hall of Fame' series, original 2/71 versions. Did not chart.

Mother/The Summer Knows
4–45471. Released 9/71. BB79.

Space Captain/One Less Bell To Answer/A House Is Not A Home
4–45511. Released 11/71. Did not chart.

The Best Thing You've Ever Done/What Are You Doing The Rest Of Your Life?
13–33207. Released 5/72. 'Hall of Fame' series, previously released tracks. Did not chart.

Sweet Inspiration/Where You Lead/Didn't We?
4–45626. Released 5/72. BB37.

Sing/Make Your Own Kind Of Music/Starting Here, Starting Now
4–45686. Released 8/72. BB94.

Didn't We?/On A Clear Day
4–45739. Released 11/72. BB82.

If I Close My Eyes/If I Close My Eyes (instrumental)
4–45780. Released 1/73. Did not chart.

The Way We Were/What Are You Doing The Rest Of Your Life?
4–45944. Released 9/73. The first song contains a different vocal take to the one on *The Way We Were* soundtrack. BB1.

The Way We Were
(Columbia Pictures promo)
No serial number. Released 9/73. Film theatres/cinema distribution only.

All In Love Is Fair/My Buddy/How About Me?
4–46024. Released 3/74. BB63.

The Way We Were/All In Love Is Fair
13–33262. Released 11/74. 'Hall of Fame' series, previously released material. Did not chart.

Guava Jelly/Love In The Afternoon
3–10075. Released 12/74. Did not chart.

Jubilation/Let The Good Times Roll
3–10130. Released 4/75. Did not chart.

How Lucky Can You Get?/More Than You Know
Arista AS 0123. Released 4/75. The A-side is an alternative version to that on the *Funny Lady* soundtrack album. Included as bonus track on CD reissue. Did not chart.

My Father's Song/By The Way
3–10198. Released 8/75. Did not chart.

Shake Me, Wake Me (When It's Over)/Widescreen
3–10272. Released 12/75. Did not chart.

Shake Me, Wake Me (short version)/**Shake Me, Wake Me** (long version)
   3–10272. Released 12/75. Promo. Arista AS 217. 12-inch promo. Did not chart. The long version runs at 4.55, the short version at 2.52.

Evergreen/I Believe In Love
   3–10450. Released 11/76. BB1.

De Reve En Reverie/Evergreen
   CBS 5101. Released 2/77. The former the French language version of 'Evergreen' was released in Canada, France and other French-speaking countries and subsequently included on the 'If I Could' Europe-only CD single, 1998.

Sempreverde/Evergreen
   CBS 5062. Released 2/77. The A-side, the Italian language version of 'Evergreen', was released only in Italian-speaking countries.

Tema De Amor De Nace Una Estrella/Creo En Amor
   CBS 5866. Released 2/77. Released in Spain with the above format, and in Argentina/Mexico with the second song performed in English. The Spanish 'Evergreen' later appeared on the 1996 US CD single 'I Finally Found Someone'.

My Heart Belongs To Me/Answer Me
   3–10555. Released 5/77. BB4.

Songbird/Honey, Can I Put On Your Clothes?
   3–10756. Released 5/78. BB25.

Prisoner/Laura and Neville (instrumental)
   3–10777. Released 7/78. Both from the film *The Eyes Of Laura Mars*. BB21.

You Don't Bring Me Flowers (with Neil Diamond)/**You Don't Bring Me Flowers** (instrumental)
  3–10840. Released 11/78. BB1.

Superman/A Man I Loved
  3–10931. Released 3/79. Did not chart.

The Main Event/Fight (short version)/ **The Main Event/Fight** (long version)
  3–11008. Released 6/79. Promo. Short version at 3.59, long at 4.51 same as soundtrack album.

No More Tears (Enough Is Enough) (with Donna Summer)/**Wet**
  1–11125. Released 10/79. The A-side is edited from the eight-minute album version that also appears on the *Memories* album. BB1.

No More Tears (Enough Is Enough) (with Donna Summer)
  Casablanca Record & Film Works NBD 20199. Released 10/79. One-sided 12-inch disco single containing 11.40 extended dance mix, also released on Summer's *On The Radio: Greatest Hits Volumes 1 & 2.*

Kiss Me In The Rain/I Ain't Gonna Cry Tonight
  1–11179. Released 12/79. BB37.

Woman In Love/Run Wild
  1–11364. Released 8/80. BB1.

Guilty (with Barry Gibb)/**Life Story**
  11–11390. Released 10/80. BB3.

What Kind Of Fool? (with Barry Gibb)/**The Love Inside**
  11–11430. Released 1/81. BB10.

Promises/Make It Like A Memory

11–2065. Released 4/81. Both sides are shortened edits from album tracks. BB48.

Promises/Make It Like A Memory

43–2089. Released 5/81. 12-inch disco single, the A-side an extended remix at 5.55 of the track on the *Guilty* album, the B-side a shorter version of the album track.

Comin' In And Out Of Your Life/Lost Inside Of You

18–2621. Released 11/81. BB11.

Memory/Evergreen

18–2717. Released 2/82. BB52.

The Way He Makes Me Feel (studio version)/The Way He Makes Me Feel (film version)

38–4177. Released 10/83. Arista AS99–1791. 12-inch promo picture disc. BB40.

Papa, Can You Hear Me?/Will Someone Ever Look At Me That Way?

38–4357. Released 1/84. The A-side has a string instrumental introduction as opposed to the chanted *chesed* on the *Yentl* album track. Did not chart.

Left In The Dark/Here We Are At Last

38–4605. Released 9/84. The A-side was not issued on album. BB50.

Left In The Dark (without spoken intro)/Left In the Dark (with spoken intro)

38–4605. Released 9/84. Promo. The A-side is an edited version of the album track at 5.28.

Make No Mistake, He's Mine (with Kim Carnes)/**Clear Sailing**
38–4695. Released 11/84. BB51.

Emotion/Here We Are At Last
38–4707. Released 2/85. The A-side is a shortened edit of the album track. BB79.

Emotion/Emotion (instrumental)
44–6167. Released 2/85. 12-inch disco single with extended remix at 6.34 of the shorter album track by Jellybean Benitez.

Somewhere/Not While I'm Around
38–5680. Released 11/85. The A-side is a shorter edit of the album track. BB43.

Send In The Clowns/Being Alive
38–5837. Released 2/86. Did not chart.

The Main Event/Fight/Promises
Columbia Mixed Masters 44H–06920. Released 2/87. 12-inch. Previously unreleased 11.42 version of the A-side, 5.55 version of the B-side.

Till I Loved You (with Don Johnson)/**Two People**
38–8062. Released 10/88. The A-side is a shortened version of album track. 38K 08062 CD 3-inch single, Streisand's first. Versions as above. CBS BARB 2 (UK) contains a 4.14 version of 'Till I Loved You'. BB25.

All I Ask Of You/On My Way To You
38–8026. Released 12/88. Did not chart.

What Were We Thinking Of?/Why Let It Go?
38–68691. Released 2/89. Vinyl and cassette only. Did not chart.

We're Not Makin' Love Anymore/Here We Are At Last
38–73016. Released 10/89. The A-side is a shortened edit of the album track. Did not chart.

You Don't Bring Me Flowers (with Neil Diamond)/**Forever In Blue Jeans** (Neil Diamond)
3-inch CD. 13K 68640. 'Hall of Fame' series, limited edition, previously released material.

The Way We Were/All In Love Is Fair
3-inch CD. 13K 68660. 'Hall of Fame' series, limited edition, previously released material.

The Music Of The Night/The Music Of The Night (both sides with Michael Crawford)
CSK5429. Released 7/93. Promo CD single. The A-side is a short version at 4.17, B-side is the track from the *Back To Broadway* album.

I've Got A Crush On You (with Frank Sinatra)/**One For My Baby** (Frank Sinatra with Kenny G)
Capitol 8–81139-2. Released 11/93. Promo CD single of edited version which appears on *Frank Sinatra: Duets*.

The Music Of The Night (with Michael Crawford)/**Children Will Listen/Move On**
Columbia/Sony Music 659738–2. Released 1/94. 'Children' contains Streisand's a cappella lullaby/monologue from the *Back To Broadway* studio sessions.

Ordinary Miracles/Ordinary Miracles (live)
38–77533. Released 5/94. Vinyl and cassette only. Did not chart.

Ordinary Miracles/As If We Never Said
Goodbye/Evergreen/Ordinary Miracles
> CD single. 44K 77534. The first song appears in both the studio version and a live version recorded 1 January 1994 at Las Vegas's MGM Grand Garden.

I Finally Found Someone (with Bryan Adams)/**Let's Make A Night To Remember** (Adams solo)/**Evergreen** (in Spanish)
> CD single. 38K 78480. Released 11/96. The duet from *The Mirror Has Two Faces*. BB8.

Tell Him (with Celine Dion)/**Everything Must Change** (Streisand solo)/**Where Is The Love?** (Dion solo)
> CD single. 665305–2. Released 11/97. The Dion solo comes from her *Let's Talk About Love* album.

If I Could/At The Same Time/I Believe (single version)/**Evergreen** (in French)
> CD single. 665522–2. Released in the Netherlands only, 2/98.

I've Dreamed Of You/At The Same Time
> CD single. 38K 79211. Released 6/99.

If You Ever Leave Me (with Vince Gill)/**Just Because/Let's Start Right Now/At The Same Time**
> CD single. 667801–2. Released in the Netherlands only, 9/99.

FILMS

Funny Girl

(Columbia Pictures, 1968, 155 mins)

Director: William Wyler. Producer: Ray Stark.
Screenplay: Isobel Lennart. Musical Tableaux:
Herbert Ross. Photography: Harry Stradling.
Sets: William Kiernan. Streisand played Fanny Brice.
With Omar Sharif, Kay Medford, Anne Francis,
Walter Pidgeon, Lee Allen, Mae Questel, Gerald
Mohr, Frank Faylen.

Hello, Dolly!

(Twentieth Century-Fox, 1969, 146 mins)

Director: Gene Kelly. Writer/producer: Ernest
Lehman, based on Thornton Wilder's novel, *The
Matchmaker*. Photography: Harry Stradling.
Sets: Walter M Scott. Streisand played Dolly Levi.
With Walter Matthau, Michael Crawford, Marianne
McAndrew, F J Peaker, Danny Lockin, Louis
Armstrong, Joyce Aymes, Tommy Tune, Fritz Feld.

On A Clear Day You Can See Forever

(Paramount, 1970, 129 mins)

>Director: Vincente Minnelli. Producer: Howard W Koch. Screenplay/lyrics: Alan Jay Lerner. Photography: Harry Stradling. Sets: George Hopkins, Ralph Bretton. Period Costumes: Cecil Beaton. Streisand played Daisy Gamble and Melinda Tentrees. With Yves Montand, Jack Nicholson, Larry Blyden, Bob Newhart, John Richardson, Pamela Brown, Simon Oakland.

The Owl And The Pussycat

(Columbia Pictures, 1970, 95 mins)

>Director: Herbert Ross. Producer: Ray Stark. Screenplay: Buck Henry, based on the play by Bill Manhoff. Photography: Harry Stradling/Andrew Laszlo. Streisand played Doris Wilgus. With George Segal, Robert Klein, Roz Kelly, Allen Garfield.

What's Up, Doc?

(Warner Bros, 1972, 97 mins)

>Director/producer: Peter Bogdanovich. Screenplay: Buck Henry, David Newman, Robert Benton from a story by Bogdanovich. Photography: Laszlo Kovacs. Sets: John Austin. Streisand played Judy Maxwell. With Ryan O'Neal, Madeleine Kahn, Austin Pendleton, Mable Albertson, Kenneth Mars, Sorrell Booke, Stefan Gierasch, Michael Murphy, Graham Jarvis, Liam Dunn.

Up The Sandbox

(First Artists, 1972, 97 mins)
>Director: Irvin Kershner. Producer: Irwin
>Winkler/Robert Chartoff. Screenplay: Paul Zindel,
>based on the novel by Anne Richardson Roiphe.
>Photography: Gordon Willis. Sets: David M Haber,
>Robert de Vestal. Streisand played Margaret
>Reynolds. With David Selby, Ariane Heller, Terry and
>Garry Smith, Paul Benedict, Jane Hoffman, Jacobo
>Morales, George Irving, Cynthia Harris, Jason Gould,
>the Sengalese Dance Company.

The Way We Were

(Columbia, 1973, 118 mins)
>Director: Sydney Pollack. Producer: Ray Stark.
>Screenplay: Arthur Laurents, based on his novel.
>Music: Marvin Hamlisch. Photography: Harry
>Stradling Jr. Sets: William Kiernan. Streisand played
>Katie Morosky. With Robert Redford, Bradford
>Dillman, Patrick O'Neal, Lois Chiles, Viveca Lindfors,
>Allyn Ann McLeries, Herb Edelman, Murray
>Hamilton, Diana Ewing, Sally Kirkland, Connie
>Forslund.

For Pete's Sake

(Columbia, 1974, 90 mins)
>Director: Peter Yates. Producers: Marty Erlichman,
>Stanley Shapiro. Screenplay: Stanley Shapiro, Maurice
>Richlin. Photography: Laszlo Kovacs. Sets: Jim Berkey.
>Streisand played Henrietta Robbins. With Michael
>Sarrazin, Estelle, Parsons, William Redfield, Molly
>Picon, Vivian Bonnell, Louis Zorich, Richard Ward.

Funny Lady

(Columbia, 1975, 140 mins)
> Director: Herbert Ross. Producer: Ray Stark.
> Screenplay: Jay Presson Allen, Arnold Schulman.
> Music: John Kander, Fred Ebb. Photography: James
> Wong Howe. Musical Tableaux: Herbert Ross.
> Streisand played Fanny Brice. With James Caan,
> Omar Sharif, Roddy McDowall, Ben Vereen, Carole
> Wells, Larry Gates, Heidi O'Rourke, Samantha
> Huffaker, Matt Emery, Gene Troobnick.

A Star Is Born

(Warner Bros, 1976, 140 mins)
> Director: Frank Pierson. Producer: Jon Peters.
> Screenplay: John Gregory Dunne, Joan Didion, Frank
> Pierson based on the story by William Wellman and
> Robert Carson. Music supervisor: Paul Williams.
> Photography: Robert Surtees. Sets: Ruby Levitt.
> Streisand played Esther Hoffman. With Kris
> Kristofferson, Paul Mazursky, Joanne Linville, Gary
> Busey, M G Kelly, Oliver Clark, Vanette Fields and
> Clydie King, Marta Heflin, Sally Kirkland, Uncle Rudy.

The Main Event

(Warner Bros, 1979, 112 mins)
> Director: Howard Zieff. Producers: Jon Peters,
> Barbra Streisand. Screenplay: Gail Parent, Andrew
> Smith. Photography: Marion Tosi. Streisand played
> Hillary Kramer. With Ryan O'Neal, Whitman Mayo,
> Paul Sand, Patti D'Arbanville, James Gregory, Chu
> Chu Malave.

All Night Long

(Universal, 1981, 99 mins)
>Director: Jean-Claude Tramont. Producer: Leonard Goldberg, Jerry Weintraub. Screenplay: W D Richter. Photography: Phillip Lathrop. Sets: Linda Spheeris. Streisand played Cheryl Gibbons. With Gene Hackman, Dennis Quaid, Kevin Dobson, Diane Ladd, William Daniels, Terry Kiser, Vernee Watson, Chris Mulkey.

Yentl

(MGM/United Artists, 1983, 134 mins)
>Director/producer: Barbra Streisand. Screenplay: Barbra Streisand, Jack Rosenthal, based on the short story by Isaac Bashevis Singer. Music: Michel Legrand. Photography: David Watkin. Streisand played Yentl and Anshel. With Mandy Patinkin, Amy Irving, Nehemiah Persoff, Steven Hill, Alan Corduner, Ruth Goring.

Nuts

(Warner Bros, 1987, 116 mins)
>Director: Martin Ritt. Producer: Barbra Streisand. Screenplay: Tom Topor, Darryl Ponicsan, Alvin Sargent, based on Topor's play. Music: Barbra Streisand. Photography: Andrzej Bartowiak. Streisand played Claudia Draper. With Richard Dreyfuss, Maureen Stapleton, Karl Malden, James Whitmore, Eli Wallach, Leslie Neilson.

The Prince Of Tides

(Columbia, 1991, 132 mins)

> Director: Barbra Streisand. Producers: Barbra Streisand, Andrew Karsch. Screenplay: Pat Conroy, Becky Johnson based on Conroy's novel. Music: James Newton Howard. Photography: Stephen Goldblatt. Sets: Caryl Heller. Streisand played Dr Susan Lowenstein. With Nick Nolte, Kate Nelligan, Blythe Danner, Jason Gould, Melinda Dillon, Jeroen Krabbe, George Carlin, Brad Sullivan.

The Mirror Has Two Faces

(TriStar Pictures, 1996, 126 mins)

> Director/producer: Barbra Streisand. Screenplay: Robert LaGravanese. Sets: John Alan Hicks. Photography: Andrzej Bartowiak. Streisand played Rose Morgan. With Jeff Bridges, Lauren Bacall, George Segal, Mimi Rogers, Pierce Brosnan, Brenda Vaccaro, Austin Pendleton, Elle Macpherson, Taina Elg.

TELEVISION PRODUCTIONS

Serving In Silence: The Margarethe Cammermeyer Story
NBC, 1995, 100 mins. With Glenn Close, Judy Davis.
Streisand was an executive producer.

Rescuers: Stories Of Courage – Two Women
Showtime, 1997, 100 mins. With Elizabeth Perkins, Fritz Weaver.
Streisand was an executive producer.

The Long Island Incident
NBC, 1998, 120 mins. With Laurie Metcalf, Mackenzie Astin.
Streisand was an executive producer.

Rescuers: Stories Of Courage – Two Couples
Showtime: 1998, 120 mins. With Linda Hamilton, Dana Delany.
Streisand was an executive producer.

Rescuers: Stories Of Courage – Two Families
Showtime: 1998. With Tim Matheson, Daryl Hannah.
Streisand was an executive producer.

STAGE PRODUCTIONS

Summer Stock

Teahouse Of The August Moon
by John Patrick
1957, Malden Bridge Playhouse, New York.
Streisand played a Japanese girl.

Picnic
by William Inge
Desk Set
by William Marchant
Same venue, same year. In the former Streisand played Millie Owens, in the latter Elsa, the secretary.

Tobacco Road
by Erskine Caldwell and Jack Kirkland
1958, Clinton Playhouse, Connecticut.
Streisand played Ellie May.

Separate Tables
by Terence Rattigan
1959, Cecilwood Theatre, Fishkill, New York.
Streisand played a British hotel resident.

The Boyfriend
by Sandy Wilson
August 16–30, 1960, same venue.
Streisand played Hortense, the maid. Her first singing role.

Off-Broadway

Purple Dust 123
by Sean O'Casey
Winter 1957–8, Cherry Lane Theatre, New York.
Streisand understudied the role of Avril.

Driftwood
by Maurice Tei Dunn
January–February 1959, Garret Theatre, New York.
Streisand played Lorna.

The Insect Comedy
by Kael and Josef Capek
8–10 May 1960, Jan Hus Theatre, New York.
Streisand played several insects.

Another Evening With Harry Stoones
Music/lyrics Jeff Harris
21 October 1961, Gramercy Arts Theatre, New York.
Streisand played two solos: 'Value' and 'Jersey'.

Broadway

I Can Get It For You Wholesale
Music/lyrics Harold Rome
22 March 1962–9 December 1962 (300 performances), Shubert Theatre, New York.
Streisand played Yetta Marmelstein.

Funny Girl
Music: Jule Styne, Lyrics: Bob Merrill
26 March 1964–26 December 1965. Winter Garden Theatre, New York.

Mimi Hines replaced Streisand as Fanny Brice and the show played until 1 July 1967, a total of 1,348 performances.

London

Funny Girl
13 April–16 July 1966, Prince of Wales Theatre.

THREE

CRITIQUE

No entertainer on the planet could have more deserved the Grammy Legend Award presented to Barbra Streisand in 1992. In a career spanning forty years she has sold over 120 million albums and her sixteen films have grossed $1.5 billion at the box-office. She has figured ten times in the *Top Ten Box Office Stars* list. She has won two Oscars, a Tony, the London Drama Critics' Award (for *Funny Girl* in 1966), ten Golden Globes (more than any other star), six *People's Choice* awards, four Georgies, the New York Drama Critics' Poll (her first award, for *I Can Get It For You Wholesale*), four Emmys and eight Grammys. Yet no singer (save perhaps Callas, whom no one ever seemed to agree over) has had such a love-hate relationship with the media. *The New York Daily News* wrote, after witnessing her first television special in 1965, 'She has the face of a bulldozer and the stridency of an ambulance siren.' Legendary songwriter Richard Rodgers, a man who certainly knew what he was talking about, wrote for the sleeve notes of one of her albums, 'Nobody is talented enough to get laughs, to bring tears, to sing with the depth of a fine cello or the lift of a climbing bird. She makes our musical world a much happier place than it was before.'

The self-professed *mieskeit* profile, too – an essential component in producing the nasal, flute-like tone of her upper register – has had its share of detractors, not least of all Streisand herself. In her acclaimed *Barbra, The Concert*, recorded in Las Vegas at the end of 1993, she amends one of the lines to Stephen Sondheim's 'I'm Still Here' – spitting out proudly, 'I've kept my nose to spite my face' and receives rapturous applause from the audience.

Describing one of her earlier performances at the Blue Angel, Robert Ruark had observed in his syndicated newspaper column, 'Her nose is more evocative of moose than Muse, and her eyes at best could be called Nilotic only by way of mascara... but when she sings "Any Place I Hang My Hat Is Home", she's beautiful, even if home is only Brooklyn.'

And *Time* magazine said of her so-called 'Egyptian' profile, which upon pain of death, emasculation or worse Streisand *never* allowed anyone to photograph from the right: 'This nose is a shrine. It starts at the summit of her hive-piled hair and ends where a trombone hits the D before Middle C. The face it divides is long and sad, and the look in repose is the essence of hound...but as she sings number after number and grows in the mind, she touches the heart with her awkwardness, her lunging number and a bravery that is all the more winning because she seems so vulnerable. People start to nudge each other and say, "This girl's *beautiful!*"'

Streisand's success is all the more remarkable because, when she began her recording career in the early 1960s, in an entertainment world dominated by rock and pop, she chose a repertoire from a list of composers and lyricists who were, commercially speaking, more or less old hat. Hoagy Carmichael, Harold Arlen and even George Gershwin, the undisputed masters of their day, were temporarily *demodé* because the modern generation were seemingly more interested in 'moon-rhymes-with-June' ditties than articulately crafted gems which were tuneful, worldly-wise and above all capable of a longevity beyond the few weeks spent in an often mundane Top 40 hit parade before being consigned to oblivion.

Mainstream radio presenters were not interested in playing the likes of 'Cry Me A River' or 'A Sleepin' Bee', save on specialist programmes which usually went out after midnight. Streisand was actually advised to stick with material which would placate the younger crowd – or at least what the media *assumed* they wanted to hear. Streisand, wisely, ignored these soothsayers. The contract she had signed was nowhere near as lucrative as it might have been had she been willing to adhere to a repertoire chosen by some unscrupulous individual interested only in making a fast buck, but it at least allowed her to sing what she wanted to sing and, surprising even herself, capture a sizeable portion of the youth market which was not interested in The Beatles, The Rolling Stones or Bob Dylan.

Inasmuch as Maria Callas had single-handedly resurrected the forgotten *bel canto* operas of the mid-18th century, so Streisand and just one other American artiste – Peggy Lee, whose career has spanned sixty years – successfully bridged the standards/rock/pop gap and brought *good* music to the masses. And even more so than Lee, with her frequently irreverent but wholly unpretentious and above all sublimely professional interpretations, Streisand had triumphed in making many of these previously neglected set-pieces her own. It is a fact that, on the extremely rare occasions when one hears her alter-ego Fanny Brice on the radio, for example, one closes one's eyes and sees Streisand.

The importance of Streisand's own musical heroines, such as Brice, and other largely ethnic antecedents such as Helen Morgan, Ruth Etting, Billie Holiday and Judy Garland, can never be overestimated. Garland aside, none had voices which would even begin to be described as technically remarkable – in their day such traits were of considerably less interest to audiences than personalities, and explains why in the days before television artistes such as Mistinguett, Eva Tanguay and Nora Bayes had such fanatical followings when basically they could not sing a note – their audiences were in search of not just glamour and good entertainment, but of someone to identify with. Quite often, the rougher the diamond, the more they had in common with the man and woman in the street, and what earned them Streisand's respect and admiration was that their frequent misery and struggles against the odds were expertly reflected in their work – even in comic songs. When Fanny Brice recorded 'My Man' and 'Second Hand Rose' she had collapsed in tears after the session – being persistently used as a doormat by the man she had been too proud to 'kick into touch' had not been fun, and when Streisand reprised this and other Depression numbers such as 'Nobody Makes A Pass At Me' she too must have been thinking about her unhappy youth – the pathos is right there in every syllable.

All of these women had battled prejudice, social injustices and sometimes a lack of the most basic human rights. Garland, Morgan and another artiste Streisand admired – Libby Holman, to whom she paid tribute with her recording of 'Moanin' Low' – in particular had spent virtually their entire careers with fingers pressed firmly on the self-destruct button. Morgan had drunk herself to death; the other two had ended their lives as suicide victims. In this respect, Streisand has overcome her own vulnerabilities – none more so than her dreadful stage fright – to stay cresting the wave, the indefatigable champion wary of overstepping the mark by becoming friendly with the demon companions of the *chanteuse-réaliste* – alcohol and opiates – though she does appear to have been acquainted with her fair share of moody, unpredictable partners. Like her predecessors earning herself the right to proclaim that whenever she sang about love or unrequited love, Streisand knew what she was singing about because she had been there, done that. This may also explain one of the reasons for her preference for the recording booth as opposed to the concert platform. It is far easier to expose one's soul and the extreme personal emotions of highly-charged numbers such as 'I Stayed Too Long At The

Fair' and 'Non, C'est Rien' within the intimacy of the studio than in front of several thousand strangers.

That Streisand remains a supreme authority of the human condition, using her celebrity status and vast wealth to champion a whole host of pressing issues, goes without saying. Another weapon in this personal vendetta against ethnic oppression is her staunch Jewishness, an innate sixth sense of survival borne of a race which has been so mercilessly, humiliatingly and needlessly hounded over the centuries. Some show business predecessors, though not ashamed of their Jewish roots, have concealed them in the same way as many gay stars have stayed in the closet for fear of castigation. From the very moment Miss Marmelstein whizzed across the stage in *I Can Get It For You Wholesale*, however, the public were made aware that here was a girl who was proud of her ancestry. In the future she would often be criticised about her work – about her religion and race, never. What better proclamation of her heritage can Streisand have bequeathed to the world than the lasting images and the score from *Yentl?* Moreover, could any Jewish entertainer but Streisand perform the Christian carol, 'Silent Night', and make every word sound so devastatingly sincere?

Streisand's strongest affinity, however, is to the gay community – thought to form a staggering seventy per cent of her fan base. Like modern day gay icons Garland, Dietrich, Piaf, Amalia Rodrigues and Callas, her strength lies with her constant, inordinate demands for nothing less than absolute perfection – often making her a nightmare to work with. Gay men, the most stigmatised of *les enfants de novembre* as they are called in France (and to whom this book is dedicated) look towards these seemingly superhuman, caring women and surrogate mother figures for strength and spiritual succour. The artistes themselves, all too frequently unhappy or insecure in their own personal relationships, instinctively feel safe amongst men who pose no threat to them, sexually. Gay fans are loyal and supportive, especially when their star's career is on the skids and 'regular' fans have deserted them. They can also be waspish, bitchy and cruel. Some of the most grotesque drag-queens imaginable have had them rolling in the aisles with their take-offs of Streisand, yet despite the epithet-laden caricatures they present – and she has seen many of these – she has never been known to complain.

On 6 October 1963, when such events were frequently broadcast live, Streisand was one of the special guests, even overshadowing the belligerent Ethel Merman, on Judy Garland's television show. Upon Garland's insistence – the older star was suffering very badly from the shakes – the pair performed what for anyone else would have been an impossible duet: Garland singing 'Get Happy' at the same time as Streisand was attacking 'Happy Days Are Here Again'. This delectable little tableau is generally regarded – with genuine heartfelt affection – as one of *the* camp moments in 60s gay musical culture. What is also interesting is that Garland, universally recognised at the time as America's greatest singing *tragédienne*, should henceforth look towards Streisand for inspiration. In 1963, when Barbra played the Coconut Grove, Garland, sitting amongst the glitterati first night audience, was so overwhelmed by what she saw and heard that she told the press, 'That's it. From now on I'm never gonna open *my* mouth again!'

While Streisand did not have any serious rivals in the United States – she really was that unique – things were much different in Europe, where similar repertoires to hers were being translated and revived by the like of Milva, Dalida, Nana Mouskouri and Petula Clark. Incredibly, most French impresarios who might have been interested in her resisted because of the first name. Another Barbara (pronounced Barr-barr-a, real name Monique Serf, 1930–97) had inherited the recently deceased Piaf's crown and eventually would surpass her, remaining the greatest female entertainer in Europe until her death. Not only was Barbara Jewish, she *looked* like Streisand, and it was rumoured in French show business circles that

Streisand had changed the spelling of her first name because she had not wanted to be confused with Barbara when she became the bigger star on the Continent – not true, of course, for the fact still remains unalterable that the French star is more important to most Europeans than Streisand will ever be.

Then had come, by way of the finicky French, an incredible stroke of luck. Piaf had left behind a small clutch of unrecorded songs and their lyricist, Michel Vaucaire (who had supplied Piaf with over thirty million-sellers, including 'Non, je ne regrette rien'), having marvelled at *The Barbra Streisand Album*, had announced, 'If Streisand's still around in two years' time, she can have her pick!' Subsequently she had been given 'Le Mur', a harrowing song which protested about the building of the Berlin Wall. Streisand's interpretation of this is so dramatically beautiful that it hurts.

Inasmuch as she had risked never getting her recording career off the ground by singing outdated standards, so too had Streisand been treading on dangerously thin ice in that she wanted to make an album of French *chansons*. She could not speak the language, therefore the words would have to be learned and pronounced phonetically, and in those days in Europe she was neither as known or as good as the artistes whose work she wanted to cover. Absolutely no one was allowed to sing a Piaf song without severe criticism, even the major French stars. Charles Trenet, a belligerent individual at the best of times, tried but failed to prevent her from singing his 'I Wish You Love', and when Lucienne Boyer heard what Streisand had done to her legendary creation, 'Parlez-Moi D'Amour', she publicly burned the album – unfairly, for this is one of its better tracks. Gilbert Becaud, on the other hand, adored her interpretation of his 'What Now My Love?', Streisand's second verse of which is nothing less than painful.

As such, the *Je M'Appelle Barbra* album, though extremely well produced and orchestrated by Michel Legrand, should have been recorded later in Streisand's career when she had more clout and when some of the better composers (Brel, Barbara, Aznavour) might have written especially for her.

Je M'Appelle Barbra, however, clearly set the precedent for musical adventure, and not all of Streisand's forays off the so-called straight and narrow would be as potentially hazardous. Her unexpected *A Christmas Album*, and the fact that the largely Jewish hierarchy at Columbia Records had allegedly frowned upon its 'gentile' segments being recorded on home ground – not that there is any record of their complaining about the huge profits they raked in.

Columbia's executives were also against Streisand's excursions away from her tried and tested show-stoppers field – the mishmash that was *What About Today?* 'I couldn't recognise my own voice', she said some years later, after hearing one of its tracks on her car radio. And is there any wonder? The Beatles' hilarious 'Honey Pie' aside – and Buffy Saint-Marie's 'Until It's Time For You To Go', which positively puts everything else on the album to shame – this was one guinea-pig most Streisand fans could well have done without, not to mention the Sarah Bernhardt cover picture.

The critical panning received by the *What About Today?* album seems to have thrown Streisand into a quandary. She had already begun work on *The Singer,* a collection of more reliable standards, and now the tracks for another, *Stoney End*, were suddenly placed under temporary embargo: should Streisand decide not to continue in the pop-contemporary direction and return to singing what her fans clearly thought she was best at, the master tapes would be destroyed in front of her to prevent bootleggers from making a killing. In the end, Streisand jumped in feet first: *The Singer* fell by the wayside and *Stoney End* surprised everyone, not least of all Streisand herself, by peaking at Number 10 on the *Billboard* chart – even though it disappointed some of her 'old' fans.

For a while, Streisand opted against casting fate to the winds too often. The standards-inspired *Barbra Joan Streisand* placated the troops and sold well, despite the inclusion of John Lennon's best forgotten 'Mother'. Much better, before her return to comparative dross with 'Butterfly', was her live *Forum* – nothing to disappoint *anyone*, here! – and *Barbra Streisand...And Other Musical Instruments*, which Jack Parnell, the doyen of British orchestra leaders, described as one of the great moments of his career – a compliment indeed from a man who generally only worked with the best.

Butterfly, generally regarded as one exercise where Streisand allowed her heart to rule her musical sensibilities by allowing someone else (Jon Peters) to push her into choosing her most unsuitable repertoire ever, remains the last truly bad Streisand album – though there would be one more potential dice with death when in 1973 she announced that she was 'going classical'.

Classical Barbra (and one thanks heaven that this was not released under its original title, *Follow The Lieder*) does not set out to prove that Streisand is a Callas or Caballe, or any other diva in the more accurate, technical sense of the word. What it does prove is that, providing the material is good, it may well be that there is nothing she cannot sing.

Again the German and Latin pieces are phonetic readings, but unlike her occasionally botched French it does not matter much here. Aside from the truly great interpreters of *lieder* – Fritz Wunderlich, Elizabeth Schwarzkopf, who *were* German – most of its other interpreters have been foreigners who likewise have often mispronounced some of the words. There seems no reason – even at almost sixty, and one may only hope – why now that her voice is more mature and malleable, she should not delight us with more of these lovely pieces in a *Classical Barbra II*.

That said, an excess of genre-bridging isn't always advisable. Though more and more musical trends are merging following the Freddie Mercury-Montserrat Caballe *Barcelona* album and the less favourable but vastly commercial couplings of The

Three Tenors with pop stars whom twenty years ago they would never have shared a stage with, let alone a recording booth, Streisand, like Pavarotti and Sinatra, has been accused of high treason by 'demoting' her talents. Namely jumping on to the duets bandwagon and embarking on a series of projects with artistes, some of whom, though hugely successful in their field, quite simply do not accord her the justice she deserves. Most of these artistes find it hard to keep up with her power and vigour, and might have been better off joining forces with their own kind. Of course, there was always the fact to consider – even if one's name happened to be Barry Gibb – that adding the name Streisand to one's curriculum vitae did wonders for one's ego and personal standing. And bank balance.

Artistically, Streisand's musical liaisons with disco diva Donna Summer and lover Don Johnson, like some of the studio-assembled later Sinatra duets and Michael Bolton's attempts at opera, were nothing short of gruesome. And when she attempts to blend her flowing, mellow tones with those of Céline Dion, an artiste who has a tendency to nauseatingly screech her upper register, one can only ask – Why?

'You Don't Bring Me Flowers', Streisand's finely woven tapestry with Neil Diamond – a singer who is very nearly her male counterpart – is, on the other hand, breathtakingly lovely and begs another question: Why record *one* song when an album would have much better sufficed?

Everyone of course, even the greatest of the superstars, makes mistakes. When not perched precariously on the pedestals where we have placed them, they are after all only human, and their often unperceived errors only make us more appreciative of this fact. On good *and* bad days, it is Streisand's artistry, fallible at times, yet supreme and omnipotent in an age of five-minute singing sensations and movie icons who cannot act, which sets her apart. Though perhaps lacking the innate 'once more with feeling' sincerity of a later Dietrich, a Piaf or a Froman whose songs were invariably autobiographically crafted to suit their complex psyches and turbulent lifestyles, Streisand's voice is nevertheless a perfectly tuned, almost technically flawless instrument and it is this which captivates, along with the spine-tingling atmosphere which is created each time she flexes her larynx – whether in the cinema, the theatre, or within the intimacy of one's living room.

On 23 January 2000, following her two Millennium concerts and whilst this book was in preparation, Barbra stunned fans with the announcement that, following two scheduled concerts in Sydney and Melbourne (her first trip to Australia) 'and 'maybe a couple more here in the States', she would be spending more time with her husband ('We just like to get in the car and go, stopping at motels and truck-stops', she said, 'We're normal people who like simple pleasures!') and would not be making any more live appearances – ever.

Speaking at the Golden Globe awards, having just received the Cecil B DeMille Lifetime Achievement Award, she added: 'I just don't like it. I don't enjoy public performances and being on a stage. Like tonight, I'm up here on a stage and my *feet* hurt! It's very hard to sing thirty songs a night. It's not fun, and I want to have *fun!* I don't enjoy public performances – public speaking, public singing, public anything. I like to be behind the camera or in a recording studio.'

As one millennium closes and another begins, and in a world sadly bereft of true superstars as opposed to fabricated commodities with which vocal and talent comes after physical attributes, let us hope, as she approaches sixty, that Barbra Streisand has at last found the great love which seems to have eluded her almost all of her life. Let us pray, however, that she changes her mind about retiring from the concert platform. We *need* her, to feel her presence within the intimacy of the auditorium, not just in the movie theatre, on television and on the hi-fi system.

To adopt a cliché, 'When they made Streisand, they sure as hell broke the mould'.

INDEX

PICTURE CREDITS